PHILIP'S

C000225283

Cycle TOURS

Dorset and Somerset

Nick Cotton

First published in 2002 by
Philip's, a division of
Octopus Publishing Group Ltd
2-4 Heron Quays
London E14 4JP

First edition 2002
First impression 2002

Based on the original Ordnance Survey Cycle Tours series
first published by Philip's and Ordnance Survey®.

ISBN 0-540-08200-7

The route maps in this book are reproduced from
Ordnance Survey® Landranger® mapping.

Text and compilation copyright © Philip's 2002

 Ordnance Survey®

This product includes mapping data licensed from Ordnance
Survey® with the permission of the Controller of Her Majesty's
Stationery Office. © Crown copyright 2002. All rights reserved.
Licence number 100011710

No part of this publication may be reproduced, stored in a
retrieval system or transmitted in any form or by any means,
electronic, mechanical, photocopying, recording or otherwise,
without the permission of the Publishers and the copyright
owners.

To the best of the Publishers' knowledge, the information in this
book was correct at the time of going to press. No responsibility
can be accepted for any error or their consequences.

The representation in this book of a road, track or path is no
evidence of the existence of a right of way.

Ordnance Survey and the OS Symbol are registered trademarks
of Ordnance Survey, the national mapping agency of Great
Britain.

Printed and bound in Spain by Cayfosa-Quebecor

Photographic acknowledgements

Comstock (Simon McBride) 111 • Nick Cotton 73, 79, 113 •
South West Water PLC 121 • Judy Todd 61, 67, 91, 117, 125 •
Andy Williams 13, 25

Contents

Abbreviations and symbols

Directions

L	left
R	right
LH	left-hand
RH	right-hand
SA	straight ahead or straight across
T-j	T-junction, a junction where you have to give way
X-roads	crossroads, a junction where you may or may not have to give way
'Placename 2'	words in quotation marks are those that appear on signposts; the numbers indicate distance in miles unless stated otherwise

Distance and grade

The number of drink bottles indicates the grade:

 Easy

 Moderate

 Strenuous

The grade is based on the amount of climbing involved.

Refreshments

Pubs and teashops on or near the route are listed. The tankard ♥ symbols indicate pubs particularly liked by the author.

Page diagrams

The page diagrams on the introductory pages show how the map pages have been laid out, how they overlap and if any inset maps have been used.

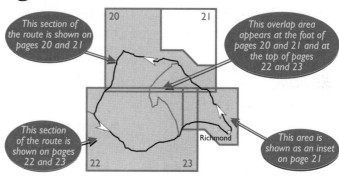

This section of the route is shown on pages 20 and 21

This overlap area appears at the foot of pages 20 and 21 and at the top of pages 22 and 23

This section of the route is shown on pages 22 and 23

This area is shown as an inset on page 21

Cross-profiles

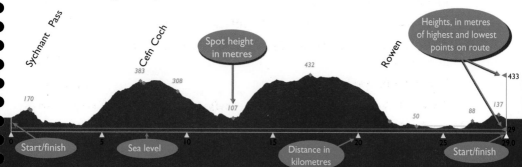

Sychnant Pass

Cefn Coch

Spot height in metres

Rowen

Heights, in metres of highest and lowest points on route

Start/finish

Sea level

Distance in kilometres

Start/finish

Legend to 1:50 000 maps

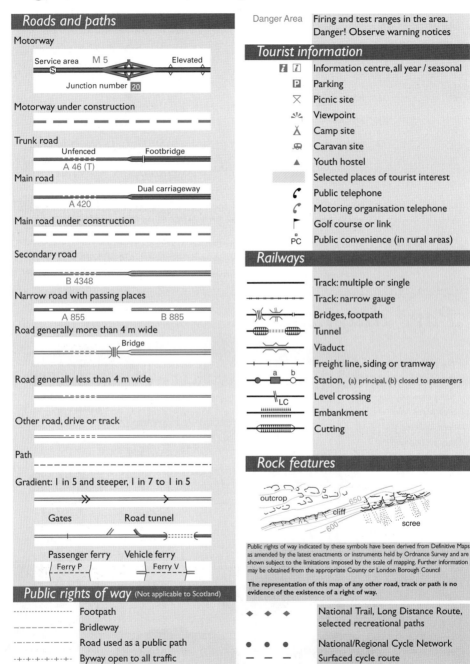

Roads and paths

Motorway

Service area — S · M 5 · Elevated
Junction number **20**

Motorway under construction

Trunk road
Unfenced · Footbridge
A 46 (T)

Main road
Dual carriageway
A 420

Main road under construction

Secondary road
B 4348

Narrow road with passing places
A 855 · B 885

Road generally more than 4 m wide
Bridge

Road generally less than 4 m wide

Other road, drive or track

Path

Gradient: 1 in 5 and steeper, 1 in 7 to 1 in 5

Gates · Road tunnel

Passenger ferry · Vehicle ferry
Ferry P · Ferry V

Public rights of way (Not applicable to Scotland)

.... Footpath
— — — — Bridleway
—·—·—·— Road used as a public path
-+-+-+-+-+- Byway open to all traffic

Danger Area — Firing and test ranges in the area. Danger! Observe warning notices

Tourist information

🛈 ⓘ	Information centre, all year / seasonal
P	Parking
✗	Picnic site
⩟	Viewpoint
Å	Camp site
⌂	Caravan site
▲	Youth hostel
▨	Selected places of tourist interest
☎	Public telephone
☎	Motoring organisation telephone
⌐	Golf course or link
PC	Public convenience (in rural areas)

Railways

———	Track: multiple or single
—+—+—	Track: narrow gauge
⧓	Bridges, footpath
▭┄▭	Tunnel
≈	Viaduct
—+—+—	Freight line, siding or tramway
●—▪—○ a b	Station, (a) principal, (b) closed to passengers
LC	Level crossing
▥	Embankment
▭	Cutting

Rock features

outcrop · —650— · cliff · —600 · scree

Public rights of way indicated by these symbols have been derived from Definitive Maps as amended by the latest enactments or instruments held by Ordnance Survey and are shown subject to the limitations imposed by the scale of mapping. Further information may be obtained from the appropriate County or London Borough Council

The representation of this map of any other road, track or path is no evidence of the existence of a right of way.

◆ ◆ ◆	National Trail, Long Distance Route, selected recreational paths
● ● ●	National/Regional Cycle Network
— — —	Surfaced cycle route

Water features

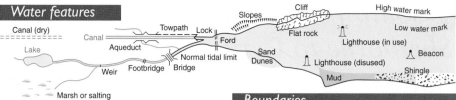

Canal (dry)
Canal
Aqueduct
Lake
Weir
Footbridge
Bridge
Towpath
Lock
Ford
Normal tidal limit
Marsh or salting

Slopes
Cliff
High water mark
Flat rock
Low water mark
Lighthouse (in use)
Sand Dunes
Lighthouse (disused)
Beacon
Mud
Shingle

General features

 Electricity transmission line (with pylons spaced conventionally)

 Pipeline (arrow indicates direction of flow)

 Buildings

 Public buildings (selected)

 Bus or coach station

 Coniferous wood

 Non-coniferous wood

 Mixed wood

 Orchard

 Park or ornamental grounds

 Quarry

Spoil heap, refuse tip or dump

Ĭ Radio or TV mast

♦ Church or chapel with tower

♦ Church or chapel with spire

+ Church or chapel without tower or spire

○ Chimney or tower

⌂ Glasshouse

╪ Graticule intersection at 5' intervals

Ⓗ Heliport

△ Triangulation pillar

Ӿ Windmill with or without sails

Ⅰ Windpump

Boundaries

+ — + — + National

-○- -○- -○- -○- London borough

National park or forest park

NT National Trust NT open access NT limited access

—·—·—·— County, region or islands area

+ + + + + District

Abbreviations

P Post office

PH Public house

MS Milestone

MP Milepost

CH Clubhouse

PC Public convenience (in rural areas)

TH Town hall, guildhall or equivalent

CG Coastguard

Antiquities

VILLA Roman

Castle Non-Roman

⚔ Battlefield (with date)

☆ Tumulus

+ Position of antiquity which cannot be drawn to scale

𝔪 Ancient monuments and historic buildings in the care of the Secretaries of State for the Environment, for Scotland and for Wales and that are open to the public

Heights

50 Contours are at 10 metres vertical interval

·144 Heights are to the nearest metre above mean sea level

Heights shown close to a triangulation pillar refer to the station height at ground level and not necessarily to the summit

South from Sherborne to Cerne Abbas

Sherborne is an attractive town close to the border of Dorset and Somerset. There is plenty to see, including two castles and an abbey, and there are lots of pubs and tea shops. The ride starts gently along quiet lanes through Bradford Abbas, Yetminster and Chetnole. The hills loom ahead and the gradual climb becomes more pronounced beyond Redford. You really feel as though you are cutting across the grain of the land as you climb up and over two ridges before swooping down into Cerne Abbas. There are lots of reasons for stopping here, not least of which is to gaze at the giant carved into the chalk. Although it is fairly busy on the ridge road, you will

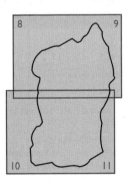

have superb views and then a fantastic descent down to Middlemarsh. Two more short climbs as the route passes through Milborne Port and you are back in Sherborne.

 Start

Tourist Information Centre, Sherborne

P Follow signs

 Distance and grade

56 km (35 miles)

Moderate/strenuous

 Terrain

The ride is divided into three parts: the flatter, northern part of Black moor Vale south of Sherborne; a very hilly middle section where you climb to the top of three ridges; and a stretch along a ridge that descends back down to Blackmoor Vale. The three major climbs are 200 m (650 ft) from Bradford Abbas to the A37 at Stagg's Folly, 97 m (320 ft) from Sydling St Nicholas to Rowden Hill and 110 m (380 ft) east from Cerne Abbas

 Nearest railway

Sherborne

Sherborne   Bradford Abbas   Yetminster   Chetnole   Redford   Frome St Quintin   Stagg's Folly   Sydling St Nicholas

Sherborne I

This small market town is full of historic buildings, notably the abbey that is now partly occupied by the famous Sherborne School. Medieval, Georgian and Victorian shopfronts line the streets but there are also remains of some Roman buildings.

Abbey Church I

The oldest surviving parts of the abbey church are the Saxon west wall and the north-west doorway; the external buttresses and south porch are Norman but much of the rest was rebuilt in the 15th-century.

Almshouse of Saint John the Baptist and John the Evangelist I

Founded in 1437, this cloister courtyard and the original stone buildings are still used as an almshouse. Shut off from the hall by a 15th-century screen is a small chapel that houses a 15th-century Flemish altar triptych.

Sherborne Old Castle 25

Very little remains of the castle built by Roger de Caen in the 11th-century. It was almost entirely reduced to ruins by Parliamentary forces in the Civil War and only the gatehouse, one of the central buildings and sections of the curtain wall survived.

Cerne Abbas II

This village is known for the Cerne Abbas Giant, a huge figure cut into the chalky hillside and believed to be a fertility figure dating from Roman times. The name Cerne Abbas derives from the Benedictine Abbey founded here in the 10th-century but only the Abbot's Porch, a 15th-century guest house and a well remain.

Sherborne New Castle 25

Constructed in the 16th-century by Sir Walter Raleigh, the last resident of the Ole Castle, the New Castle stands on a hill on the other side of the river in grounds laid out by 'Capability' Brown. Sir John Digby acquired the estate in 1617 and added the turreted wings and the Digby family crest wherever possible; the estate has belonged to the family ever since. Very little of the original interior survived extensive 'Jacobean-style' redecoration in the 19th-century: only the Georgian library and the Jacobean oak-pan-elled room remain.

Cerne Abbas

Middlemarsh

Holt Hill

Goathill

Oborne

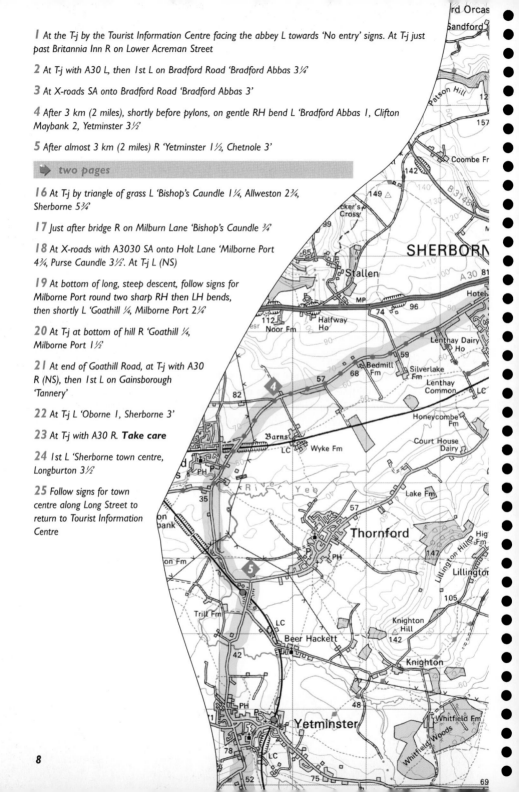

1 At the T-j by the Tourist Information Centre facing the abbey L towards 'No entry' signs. At T-j just past Britannia Inn R on Lower Acreman Street

2 At T-j with A30 L, then 1st L on Bradford Road 'Bradford Abbas 3¼'

3 At X-roads SA onto Bradford Road 'Bradford Abbas 3'

4 After 3 km (2 miles), shortly before pylons, on gentle RH bend L 'Bradford Abbas 1, Clifton Maybank 2, Yetminster 3½'

5 After almost 3 km (2 miles) R 'Yetminster 1½, Chetnole 3'

➡ *two pages*

16 At T-j by triangle of grass L 'Bishop's Caundle 1¼, Allweston 2¾, Sherborne 5¾'

17 Just after bridge R on Milburn Lane 'Bishop's Caundle ¾'

18 At X-roads with A3030 SA onto Holt Lane 'Milborne Port 4¾, Purse Caundle 3½'. At T-j L (NS)

19 At bottom of long, steep descent, follow signs for Milborne Port round two sharp RH then LH bends, then shortly L 'Goathill ¼, Milborne Port 2¼'

20 At T-j at bottom of hill R 'Goathill ¼, Milborne Port 1½'

21 At end of Goathill Road, at T-j with A30 R (NS), then 1st L on Gainsborough 'Tannery'

22 At T-j L 'Oborne 1, Sherborne 3'

23 At T-j with A30 R. **Take care**

24 1st L 'Sherborne town centre, Longburton 3½'

25 Follow signs for town centre along Long Street to return to Tourist Information Centre

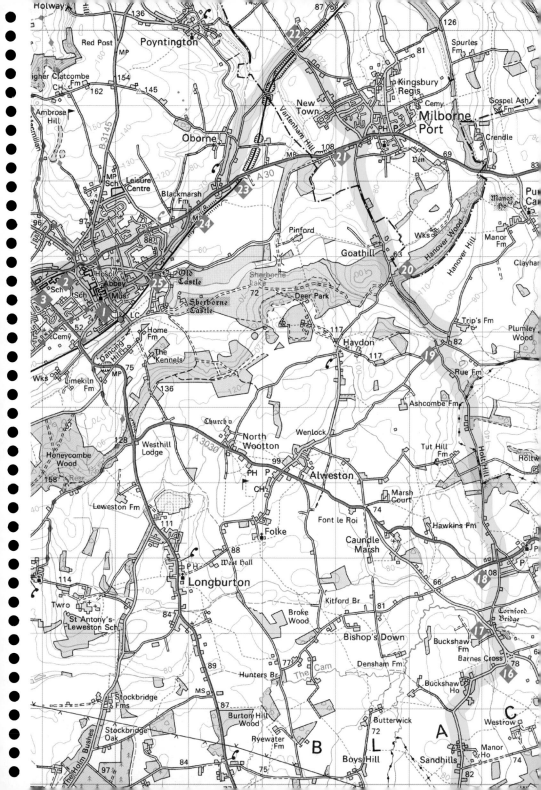

6 Follow signs for Chetnole past Yetminster. Follow signs for Melbury Bubb out of Chetnole

7 Do not turn off to Melbury Bubb. Continue to T-j, turn R 'Evershot 2¾'

8 At T-j R 'Evershot 1½'. At T-j with A37 L 'Dorchester', then 1st R 'Frome St Quintin 1, Chantmarle 1¾'

9 After 4 km (2½ miles), at T-j by triangle of grass L 'Sydling St Nicholas, Cerne Abbas'

10 At T-j with A37 SA through gate onto disused road.
At T-j L (NS)

11 Descend to ford near Sydling St Nicholas, climb then descend to Cerne Abbas. At X-roads with A352 SA 'Village Centre, Buckland Newton 5'

12 Through village and climb steeply to ridge. At T-j L 'Buckland Newton 3, Sherborne 10'

13 Short further climb, fine long descent. This road may be busy. Follow signs for Middlemarsh. In Middlemarsh just before A352 R at X-roads (NS)

14 At T-j L 'Glanvilles Wotton ¼, Sherborne 7'

15 Shortly on LH bend by a memorial stone R 'Holwell 2½, Bishop's Caundle 3¾'

◀ two pages

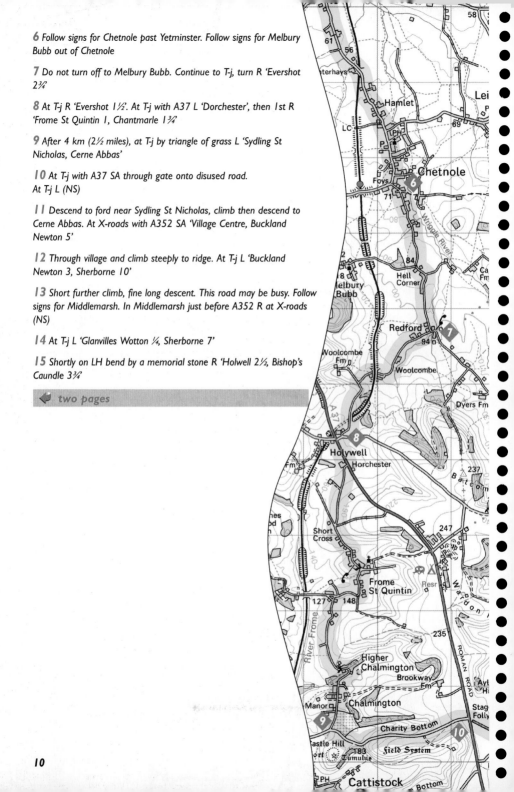

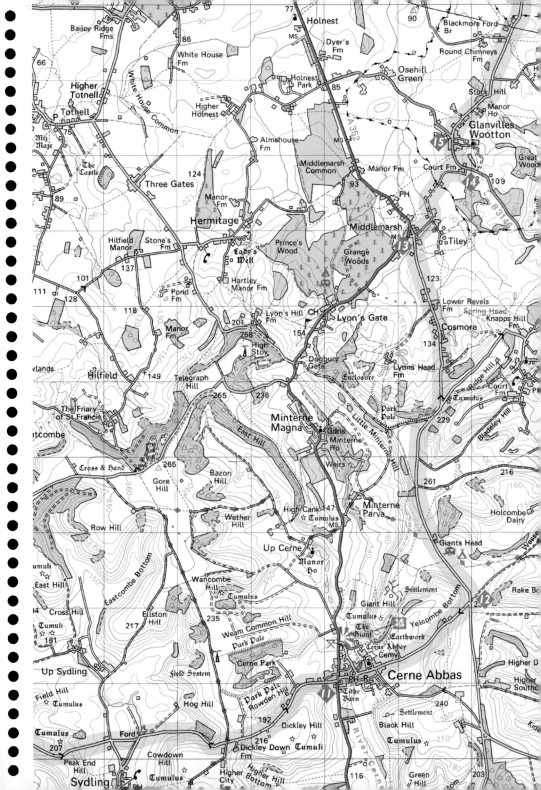

From Sturminster Newton over Bulbarrow Hill to Milton Abbas

Starting from the quiet charm of the small town of Sturminster Newton, the ride passes through the attractive villages of Child Okeford and Okeford Fitzpaine before the first ascent of Bulbarrow Hill. At

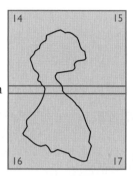

almost 270 m (900 ft), Bulbarrow is the highest point in Dorset, and the views, particularly to the northwest over the Vale of Blackmoor, are spectacular. This ride gives you a double dose of Bulbarrow, with a lovely long descent through the shallow valley of the River Winterborne. The village of Milton Abbas is quite extraordinary in its precise picturesqueness, exact rows of thatched cottages set against a wooded backdrop.

Start

The Swan Hotel, Sturminster Newton

P Station Road, off the B3091 Shaftesbury Road

Distance and grade

44 km (28 miles)

🠖🠖🠖 Moderate

Terrain

Two major climbs, both towards the ridge of Bulbarrow Hill. The first, of 150 m (500 ft), lies south from Okeford Fitzpaine; the second is in two stages, from Winterborne Whitechurch to Milton Abbas (100 m, 340 ft) then from Milton to the viewpoint (130 m, 430 ft)

Nearest railway

Gillingham, 13 km (8 miles) north of Sturminster Newton, or Wool, 14 km (9 miles) south of Winterborne Whitechurch

Sturminster Newton

Manston

Child Okeford

Shillingstone

Okeford Fitzpaine

Bulbarrow Hill Ridge

Winterborne Stickland

Refreshments

Lots of choice in **Sturminster Newton**
Saxon Arms PH 🍺🍺, Baker Arms PH, **Child Okeford**
Royal Oak PH, **Okeford fitzpaine**
Shire Horse PH, **Winterborne Stickland**
Milton Arms PH, **Winterborne Whitechurch**
Hambro Arms PH 🍺🍺, **Milton Abbas**

▼ Milton Abbas

Winterborne Whitechurch   Milton Abbas   Hilton   Bulbarrow Hill Ridge   Belchalwell   The Common

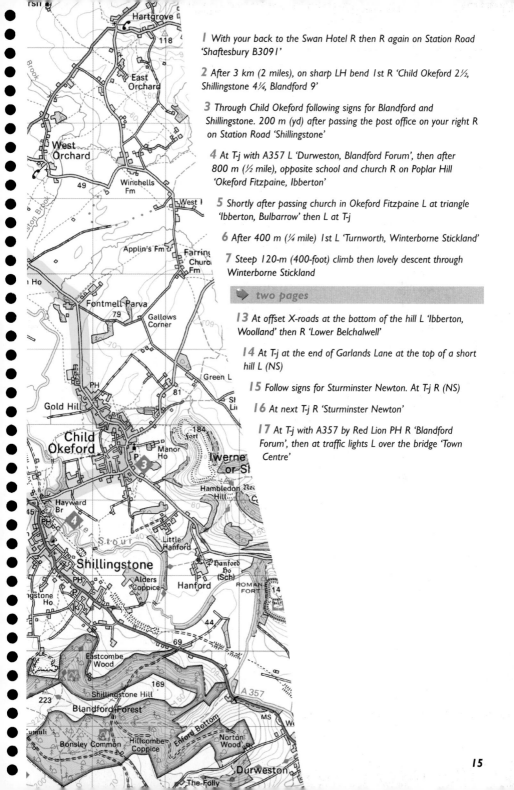

1 With your back to the Swan Hotel R then R again on Station Road 'Shaftesbury B3091'

2 After 3 km (2 miles), on sharp LH bend 1st R 'Child Okeford 2½, Shillingstone 4¼, Blandford 9'

3 Through Child Okeford following signs for Blandford and Shillingstone. 200 m (yd) after passing the post office on your right R on Station Road 'Shillingstone'

4 At T-j with A357 L 'Durweston, Blandford Forum', then after 800 m (½ mile), opposite school and church R on Poplar Hill 'Okeford Fitzpaine, Ibberton'

5 Shortly after passing church in Okeford Fitzpaine L at triangle 'Ibberton, Bulbarrow' then L at T-j

6 After 400 m (¼ mile) 1st L 'Turnworth, Winterborne Stickland'

7 Steep 120-m (400-foot) climb then lovely descent through Winterborne Stickland

➡ *two pages*

13 At offset X-roads at the bottom of the hill L 'Ibberton, Woolland' then R 'Lower Belchalwell'

14 At T-j at the end of Garlands Lane at the top of a short hill L (NS)

15 Follow signs for Sturminster Newton. At T-j R (NS)

16 At next T-j R 'Sturminster Newton'

17 At T-j with A357 by Red Lion PH R 'Blandford Forum', then at traffic lights L over the bridge 'Town Centre'

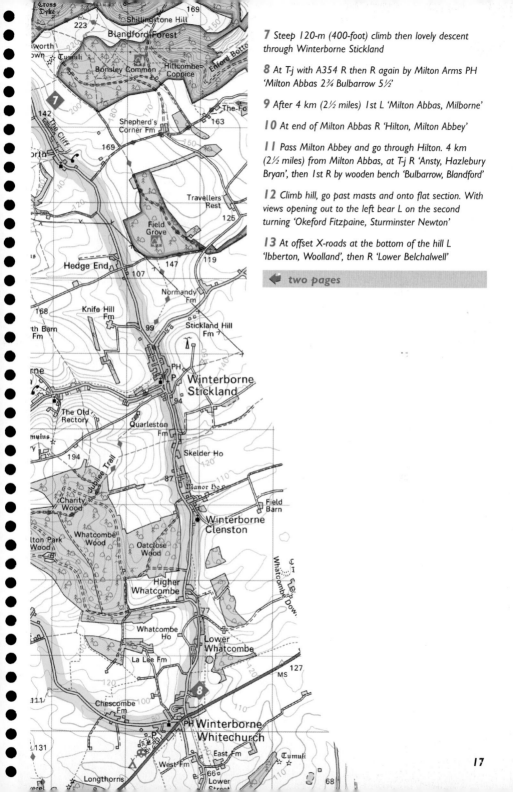

7 Steep 120-m (400-foot) climb then lovely descent through Winterborne Stickland

8 At T-j with A354 R then R again by Milton Arms PH 'Milton Abbas 2¾ Bulbarrow 5½'

9 After 4 km (2½ miles) 1st L 'Milton Abbas, Milborne'

10 At end of Milton Abbas R 'Hilton, Milton Abbey'

11 Pass Milton Abbey and go through Hilton. 4 km (2½ miles) from Milton Abbas, at T-j R 'Ansty, Hazlebury Bryan', then 1st R by wooden bench 'Bulbarrow, Blandford'

12 Climb hill, go past masts and onto flat section. With views opening out to the left bear L on the second turning 'Okeford Fitzpaine, Sturminster Newton'

13 At offset X-roads at the bottom of the hill L 'Ibberton, Woolland', then R 'Lower Belchalwell'

← **two pages**

Chalk downland and river valleys through three counties

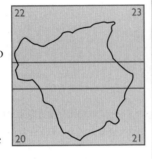

Passing though Hampshire and Dorset, this ride also takes in a slice of Wiltshire to form a lovely circuit over the chalk downs and along the Ebble Valley. Starting in the small village of Cranborne, it crosses two ridges, with especially fine views from the second one on Knowle Hill. The ride descends into the Ebble Valley at Broad Chalke and gently climbs through the charming villages of Ebbesborne Wake, Alvediston and Berwick St John. The big climb nearly to the top of Win Green lies ahead. You can now feast your eyes on the magnificent views all around and look forward to a gentle descent almost all the way to Gussage All Saints and only a gentle rise back to Cranborne.

 Start

The Sheaf of Arrows PH, Cranborne, on the B3078 between Fordingbridge and Wimborne Minster

P In Water Street, off the road to Damerham, near the fire station

 Distance and grade

52 km (33 miles)

Moderate

 Terrain

Three climbs, the first one out of the Crane Valley to Martin Wood (85 m, 280 ft), the second from Martin over Knowle Hill (140 m, 465 ft) and the last and longest from Broad Chalke, gently then more steeply up to Ashmore Down, beneath Win Green (190 m, 630 ft)

 Nearest railway

Tisbury, 8 km (5 miles) from the route at Alvediston

Cranborne   Martin Wood   Tidpit   Martin   Knowle Hill   Broad Chalke   Fifield Bavant   Ebbesborne Wake   Alvediston   Berwick St John

Places of interest

Cranborne Manor Gardens 1

Laid out in the 17th-century, these gardens contain some very interesting plants. There is a pergola walk, a church walk, a herb garden and a river garden with borders full of unusual bulbs. A Jacobean mount garden looks down to a small garden containing 16th- and 17th-century flowers.

Refreshments

Fleur de Lys PH 📖📖, *Sheaf of Arrows PH,*
Cranborne
Queens Head PH 📖, **Broad Chalke**
Horseshoes Inn 📖📖, **Ebbesbourne Wake**
Talbot Inn 📖, **Berwick St John**
King John PH, **Tollard Royal**
Drovers Inn 📖📖, **Gussage All Saints**

Cranborne Chase 14–15

This large area of grassland and beechwoods was once a royal hunting forest before the hunting rights passed to the earls of Salisbury and Shaftesbury.

Chettle House 18

Slightly off the route, this house was built by Thomas Archer in 1710 and although much of it has been modified, the staircase remains as a fine example of English Baroque architecture.

Ashmore Down

Tollard Royal

Farnham

Gussage All Saints

Wimborne St Giles

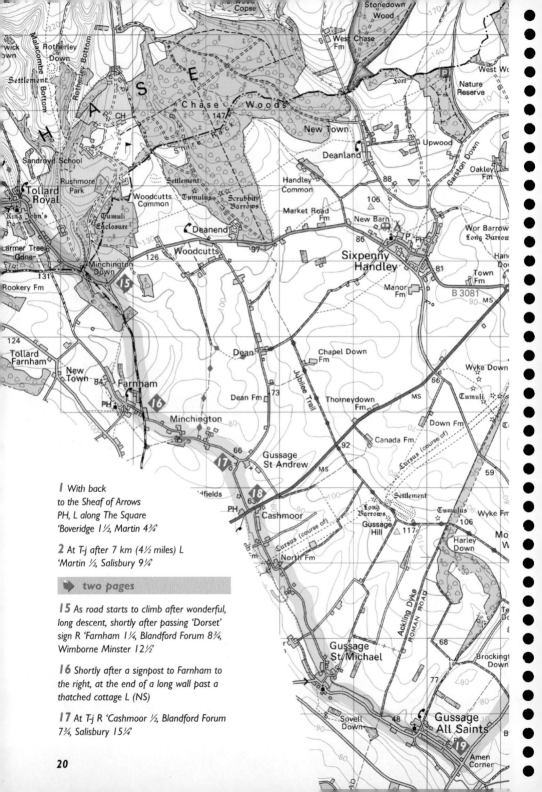

1 With back
to the Sheaf of Arrows
PH, L along The Square
'Boveridge 1½, Martin 4¾'

2 At T-j after 7 km (4½ miles) L
'Martin ½, Salisbury 9¼'

➡ **two pages**

15 As road starts to climb after wonderful,
long descent, shortly after passing 'Dorset'
sign R 'Farnham 1¼, Blandford Forum 8¾,
Wimborne Minster 12½'

16 Shortly after a signpost to Farnham to
the right, at the end of a long wall past a
thatched cottage L (NS)

17 At T-j R 'Cashmoor ½, Blandford Forum
7¾, Salisbury 15¼'

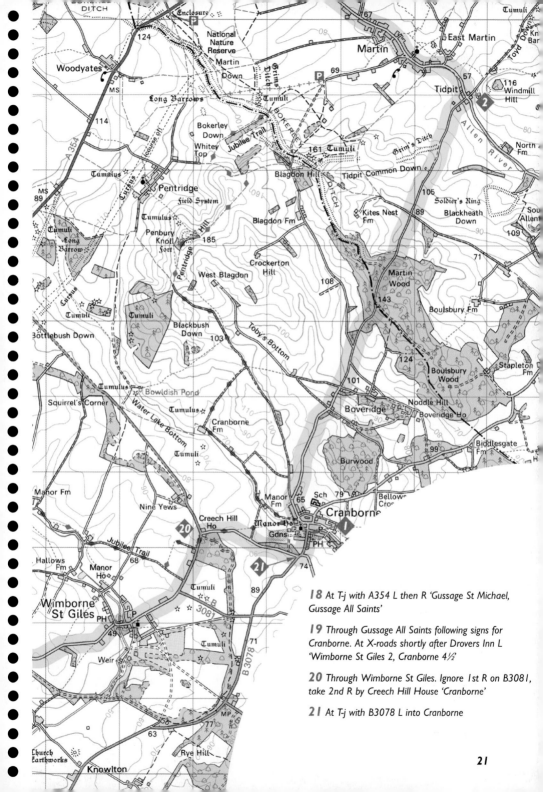

18 At T-j with A354 L then R 'Gussage St Michael, Gussage All Saints'

19 Through Gussage All Saints following signs for Cranborne. At X-roads shortly after Drovers Inn L 'Wimborne St Giles 2, Cranborne 4½'

20 Through Wimborne St Giles. Ignore 1st R on B3081, take 2nd R by Creech Hill House 'Cranborne'

21 At T-j with B3078 L into Cranborne

3 *Take care.* At X-roads with A354 dual carriageway SA 'Broad Chalke 3½'

4 *Climb then descend.* 5½ km (3½ miles) after crossing the A354, shortly after the village sign for Broad Chalke and just before a 'Children's Playground' sign turn L 'Bowerchalke, Shaftesbury'

5 At T-j by church L 'Bowerchalke' (or R for PH)

6 At end of village by a small triangle of grass R

7 After short, steep hill at T-j L

8 Follow signs for Ebbesborne Wake and 'Village' past Three Horseshoes PH

9 At T-j L 'Shaftesbury'

10 In Berwick St John past the Talbot Inn bear R on Church Street 'Shaftesbury A30'

11 After 3 km (2 miles), and just **before** A30 L '7.5T except for access'

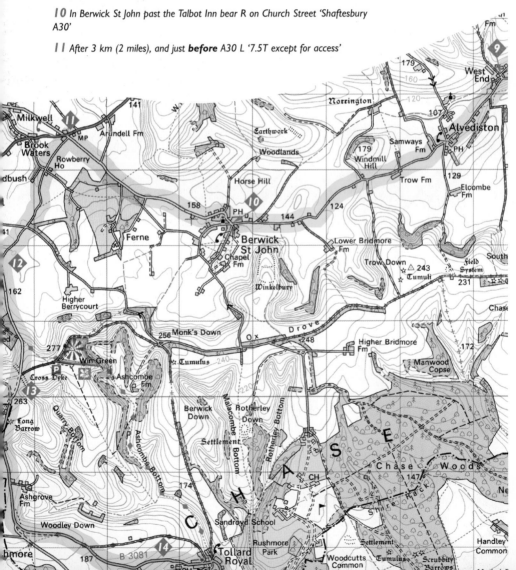

12 *SA through two X-roads (your priority). At T-j L 'Tollard Royal, Farnham'*

13 *110 m (380 ft) climb. Fine views. At X-roads L 'Tollard Royal, Ringwood'*

14 *Follow the road for 5½ km (3½ miles) passing through Tollard Royal*

◀ *three pages*

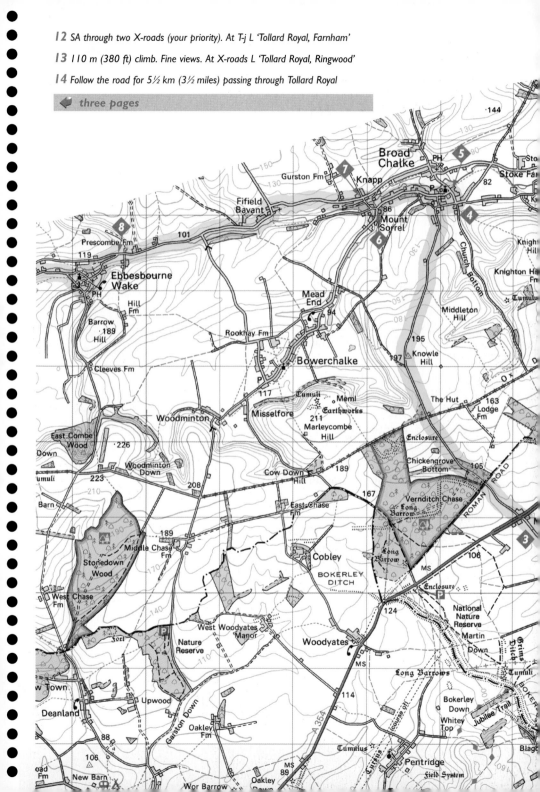

From Blandford Forum to Wimborne Minster via the Tarrant and Stour valleys

The elegant Georgian appearance of Blandford Forum is the result of a fire that devastated the centre of town in the summer of 1731. The town was rebuilt by the Bastard Brothers. The ride goes north, then east to cross the hills separating the valleys of the rivers Stour and Tarrant. The Tarrant, really little more than a stream, gives rise to no fewer than eight hamlets and villages named after it in a stretch of 13 km (8 miles). The route joins the valley at the first of these, Tarrant Gunville, and proceeds via Tarrant Hinton, Launceston and Monkton before leaving the valley, climbing The Cliff and proceeding to the attractive market town of Wimborne Minster. The return is on quiet, delightful lanes close to the River Stour, with the opportunity of a fine tea stop near Tarrant Crawford.

Start

Tourist Information Centre, Blandford Forum

🅿 Adjacent to the Tourist Information Centre

Distance and grade

48 km (30 miles)

Easy

Terrain

One long, steady climb of 91 m (300 ft) between Blandford Forum and Tarrant Gunville, a short steep climb out of the Tarrant Valley, otherwise very easy gradients

Nearest railway

Poole, 10 km (6 miles) south of Wimborne Minster

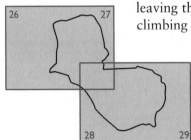

▲ Wimborne Minster

Refreshments

Greyhound PH 🍷, plenty of choice in **Blandford Forum**
Bugle Horn PH 🍷, **Tarrant Gunville**
Langton Arms PH 🍷🍷, **Tarrant Monkton**
Stocks Inn, **Furzehill**
White Hart PH 🍷, Rising Sun PH 🍷, plenty of choice,
Wimborne Minster
Anchor Inn, **Shapwick**
Keyneston Mill tea shop, near **Tarrant Crawford**

Wimborne Minster

Shapwick

1 With your back to the Tourist Information Centre R on Salisbury Street following signs for Salisbury and one-way system to L at 1st traffic lights. Stay in middle lane at 2nd traffic lights

2 Climb out of town past Police Station and District Council offices. After 1 km (¾ mile), shortly after D'Amory Arms PH on your right and just before church on your left turn L 'Melbury Abbas, Shaftesbury, Industrial Estate'

3 At roundabout with A354 SA 'Sunrise Business Park, Melbury Abbas 8'

4 Following signs for Melbury and Shaftesbury, after 4 km (2½ miles) 2nd R (shortly after Paradise Farm Stud on your right) 'Tarrant Gunville'

5 In Tarrant Gunville at T-j R 'Tarrant Hinton 1½, Blandford Forum 6, Salisbury 19'

6 At T-j with A354 R 'Blandford', then L 'Tarrant Launceston 1, Tarrant Monkton 1½'

7 In Tarrant Monkton, on sharp LH bend, turn R through ford towards Langton Arms PH. Go past church and PH. At T-j R 'Tarrant Rawston, Rushton, Keyneston'

8 After 2 km (1¼ miles) 1st L sharply back on yourself 'Witchampton'. (**Or** SA for shorter route)

➡ two pages

19 At T-j with A354 L onto pavement and through underpass by the river. Follow this road (Langton Road) to the end

20 At T-j L following signs for Dorchester to return to Tourist Information Centre

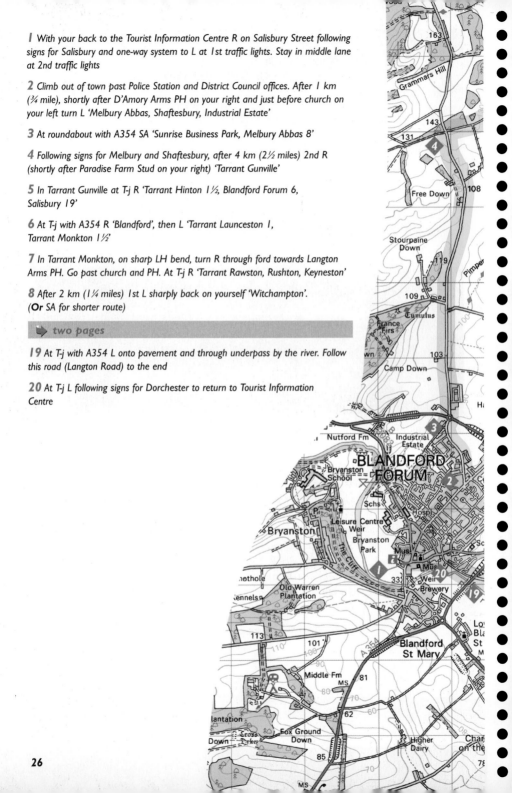

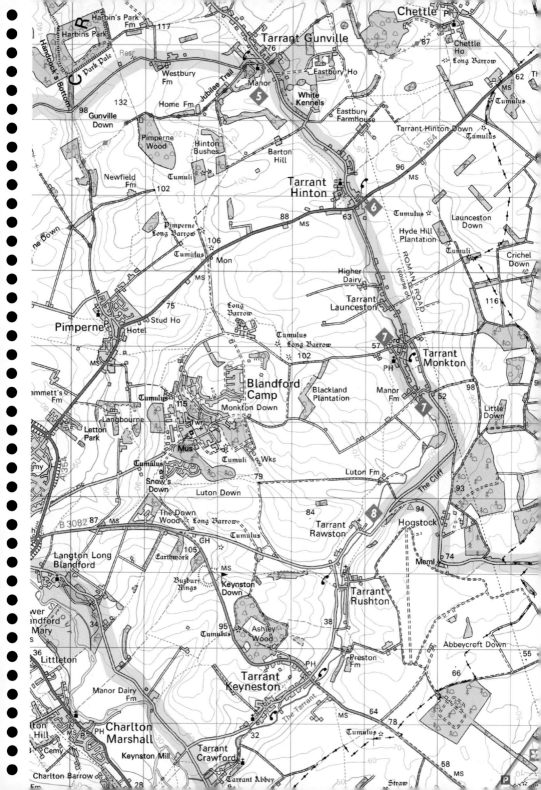

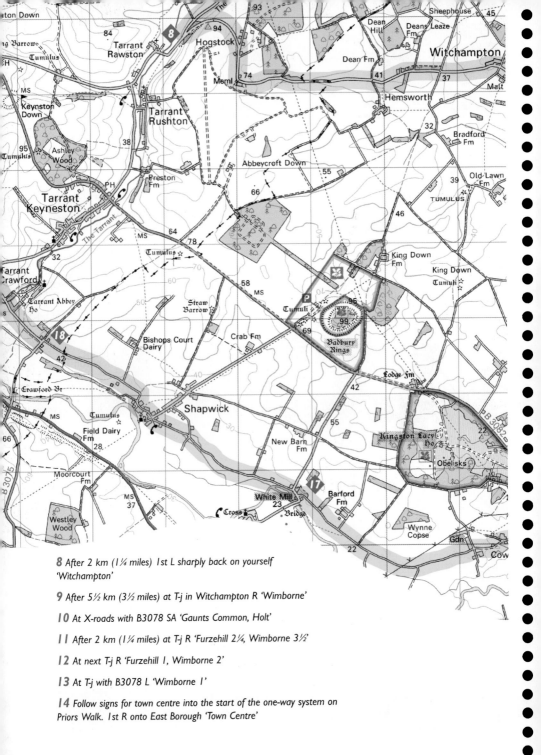

8 *After 2 km (1¼ miles) 1st L sharply back on yourself 'Witchampton'*

9 *After 5½ km (3½ miles) at T-j in Witchampton R 'Wimborne'*

10 *At X-roads with B3078 SA 'Gaunts Common, Holt'*

11 *After 2 km (1¼ miles) at T-j R 'Furzehill 2¼, Wimborne 3½'*

12 *At next T-j R 'Furzehill 1, Wimborne 2'*

13 *At T-j with B3078 L 'Wimborne 1'*

14 *Follow signs for town centre into the start of the one-way system on Priors Walk. 1st R onto East Borough 'Town Centre'*

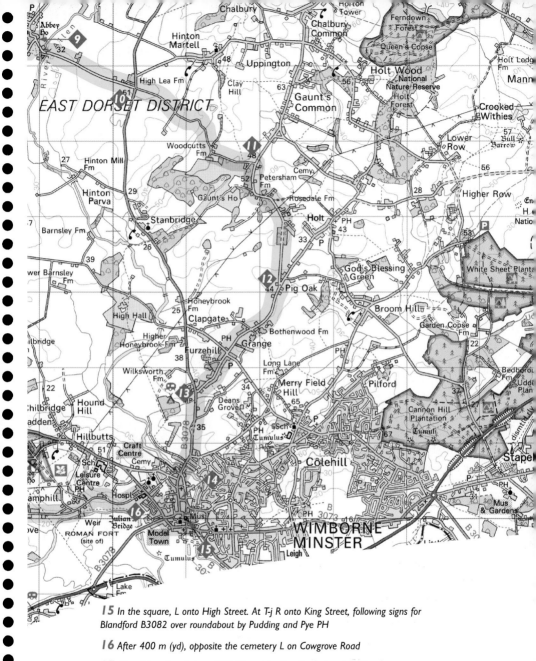

15 In the square, L onto High Street. At T-j R onto King Street, following signs for Blandford B3082 over roundabout by Pudding and Pye PH

16 After 400 m (yd), opposite the cemetery L on Cowgrove Road

17 After 5 km (3 miles), at T-j R 'Shapwick, Crawford', then L (NS)

18 2½ km (1½ miles) after passing Anchor Inn in Shapwick 1st R by memorial cross 'Blandford Forum'

👈 *three pages*

5 Southwest from Dorchester to Abbotsbury and along the top of the Downs

Start

The roundabout at the west end of High Street West, Dorchester

P Follow signs

Distance and grade

57 km (36 miles)

Moderate/ strenuous

Terrain

Out of the Frome Valley, over the hills and along the coast, down into the valley of the River Bride, up and over the hills to drop into the Frome Valley again. Three major climbs: 76 m (250 ft) south of Winterborne Monkton, 180 m (600 ft) from Abbotsbury west to the Fort, 230 m (750 ft) between Swyre and Eggardon Hill

Nearest railway

Dorchester

Dorchester is a bustling county town with plenty of interest, but it is nevertheless very easy to escape from into the countryside. The ride takes you south out of town along the southern edge of the

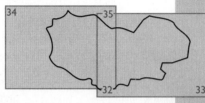

imposing earthworks of Maiden Castle and through the delightful stone-and-thatch hamlet of Friar Waddon, and enters Abbotsbury the back way via the Swannery. Abbotsbury offers many excuses for stopping, both visual and gastronomic. You will need plenty of energy to get up the hill out of Abbotsbury. Depending on the season, the road may be busy but the views out to sea justify the climb. All the height is lost on a lovely long descent into Swyre and down to cross the River Bride. The longest climb now starts and will take you up to the top of Eggardon Hill. You could, of course, break your journey at the Spyway Inn. From the trig point at the top, a long gentle descent of several miles, with views to both sides, drops you close to the A35. This very busy road is avoided by heading north to Muckleford and following the Frome Valley back into Dorchester.

Dorchester · Winterborne Monkton · Coryates · Rodden · Abbotsbury · fort · Swy

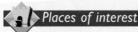
Dorchester 1

Originally an important Roman town, Dorchester has some interesting remains although much was destroyed in a fire in 1613. A 4th-century town house has been excavated and the Roman layout of the town influenced the modern street plan. The Monmouth Rebellion and the Tolpuddle Martyrs were also connected with Dorchester; the notorious trial of the participants in the former took place in the Antelope Hotel and the latter were condemned to transportation in the Shire Hall further along the High Street. Thomas Hardy brought fame to Dorchester as the setting of many of his novels (calling it Casterbridge) and the streets of Georgian and Victorian houses are easily recognisable from his books. He was born in a village nearby and worked as an apprentice architect in the town; the Dorset County Museum contains much about him.

Refreshments

Lots of choice in **Dorchester**
Elm Tree PH 🍽🍷*, just off the route,*
Langton Herring
Ilchester Arms PH 🍽🍷*,* **Abbotsbury**
Bull Inn PH, **Swyre**
The Spyway PH 🍽🍷*,* **Askerwell**

Abbotsbury 10

An ancient Benedictine monastery stood here but only a 12th-century wall and a large 15th-century tithe barn remain. The Church of St Nicholas has bullet marks from the Civil War. Nearby, the Abbotsbury Gardens occupy a sheltered spot, free from frost, which has an almost sub-tropical climate. The plants grown, especially the trees, are appropriate to the unusual climate and there is a great variety of flowers. A swannery lies to the south of the village and was established by the monks in the late 14th-century to provide food for the monastery and the village; it is now the home of over 500 swans as well as wild geese, ducks and other water birds.

Nine Stones, Winterbourne Abbas 19

Slightly off the route, this ancient stone circle is the most important in the area.

Sun. May 5th 2002
Fantastic ride. Marvellous views
"Scephred Isle". Jewel in silver sea
Yellowhammers. Saw larks
Chilcombe lunch at Ilchester Arms
36 m. Missed out Dorchester
Charminster — W St. Martins — Char.
(Staying at Inn for All Seasons)
Charminster charming stay?

Chilcombe
Askerswell
Spyway
Eggardon Hill

Knowle Hill
Muckleford
Bradford Peverell

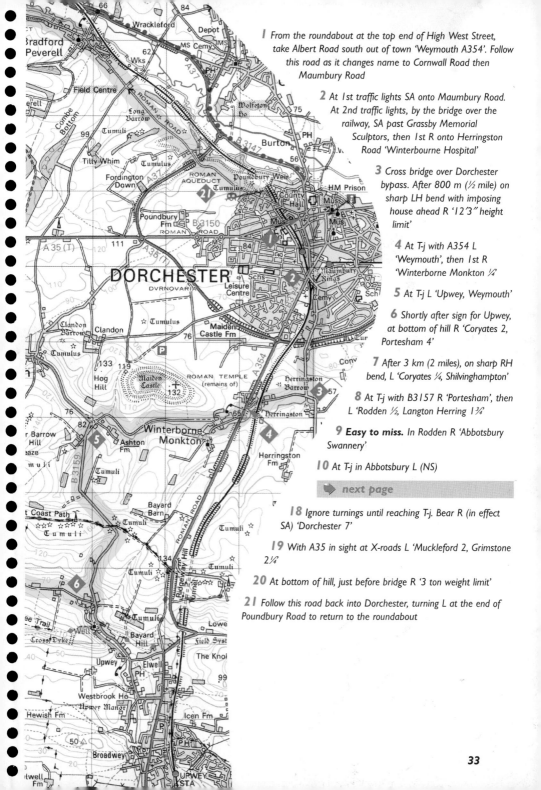

1 From the roundabout at the top end of High West Street, take Albert Road south out of town 'Weymouth A354'. Follow this road as it changes name to Cornwall Road then Maumbury Road

2 At 1st traffic lights SA onto Maumbury Road. At 2nd traffic lights, by the bridge over the railway, SA past Grassby Memorial Sculptors, then 1st R onto Herringston Road 'Winterbourne Hospital'

3 Cross bridge over Dorchester bypass. After 800 m (½ mile) on sharp LH bend with imposing house ahead R '12′3″ height limit'

4 At T-j with A354 L 'Weymouth', then 1st R 'Winterborne Monkton ¼'

5 At T-j L 'Upwey, Weymouth'

6 Shortly after sign for Upwey, at bottom of hill R 'Coryates 2, Portesham 4'

7 After 3 km (2 miles), on sharp RH bend, L 'Coryates ¼, Shilvinghampton'

8 At T-j with B3157 R 'Portesham', then L 'Rodden ½, Langton Herring 1¾'

9 Easy to miss. In Rodden R 'Abbotsbury Swannery'

10 At T-j in Abbotsbury L (NS)

➡ next page

18 Ignore turnings until reaching T-j. Bear R (in effect SA) 'Dorchester 7'

19 With A35 in sight at X-roads L 'Muckleford 2, Grimstone 2¼'

20 At bottom of hill, just before bridge R '3 ton weight limit'

21 Follow this road back into Dorchester, turning L at the end of Poundbury Road to return to the roundabout

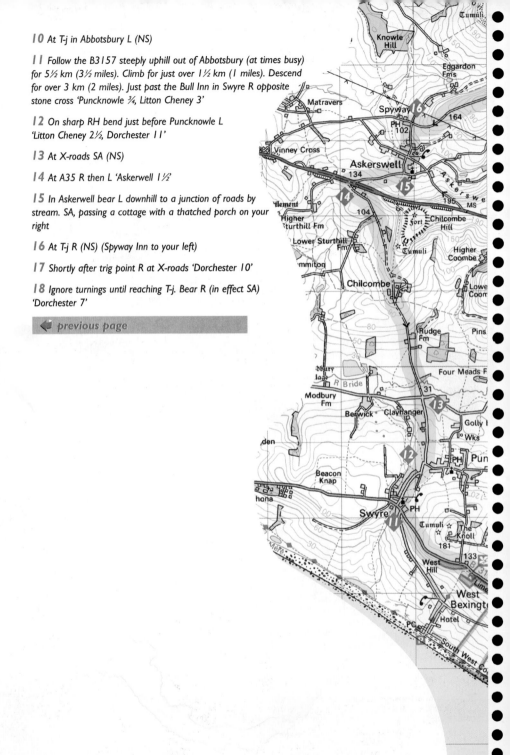

10 At T-j in Abbotsbury L (NS)

11 Follow the B3157 steeply uphill out of Abbotsbury (at times busy) for 5½ km (3½ miles). Climb for just over 1½ km (1 miles). Descend for over 3 km (2 miles). Just past the Bull Inn in Swyre R opposite stone cross 'Puncknowle ¾, Litton Cheney 3'

12 On sharp RH bend just before Puncknowle L 'Litton Cheney 2½, Dorchester 11'

13 At X-roads SA (NS)

14 At A35 R then L 'Askerwell 1½'

15 In Askerwell bear L downhill to a junction of roads by stream. SA, passing a cottage with a thatched porch on your right

16 At T-j R (NS) (Spyway Inn to your left)

17 Shortly after trig point R at X-roads 'Dorchester 10'

18 Ignore turnings until reaching T-j. Bear R (in effect SA) 'Dorchester 7'

◀ previous page

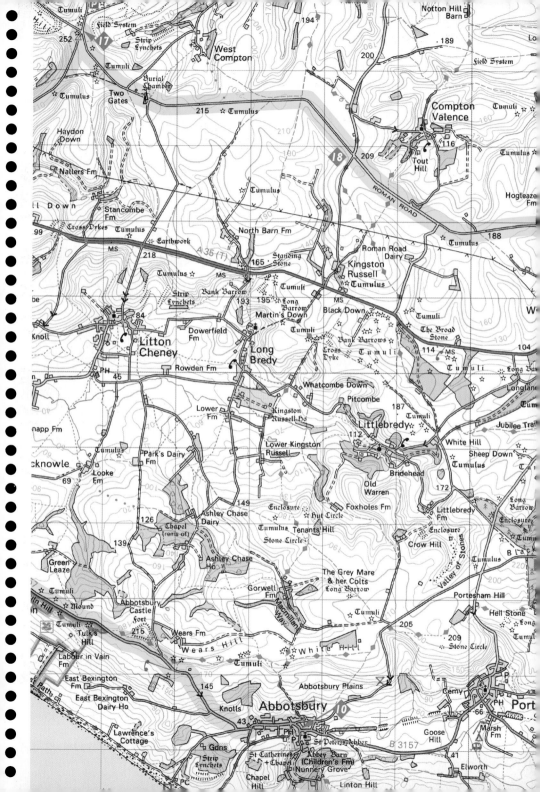

Through west Dorset hills from Bridport to Beaminster and Rampisham

A challenging ride through the beautiful crumpled green landscape of west Dorset. With a never-ending supply of hills, this is not a route for the faint-hearted. However, the quiet lanes and magnificent views, the charm of villages such as Stoke Abbott and Powerstock, and the variety of watering holes in Beaminster make it a thoroughly satisfying tour. The climb from Beaminster is very tough, so be aware of this on your second helping of chocolate fudge cake.

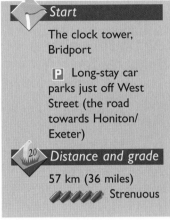

Perhaps you will prefer to walk. The views from the ridge above Corscombe are worth the climb, but the best is still to come: the stretch of road along the north side of Eggardon Hill must be one of the most beautiful in all of southern England.

Bridport   Moorbath   Broadoak   Monkwood   Stoke Abbott   Beaminster   Corscombe

Terrain

Over 760 m (2500 ft) of climbing, with three major hills: 120 m (400 ft) to the ridge west of Stoke Abbott, 180 m (600 ft) from Beaminster northeast towards Corscombe and 140 m (450 ft) from Toller Porcorum to Eggardon Hill

Nearest railway

Crewkerne, 10 km (6 miles) north of Beaminster

Refreshments

George PH 🍴🍴, lots of choice in **Bridport**
Ilchester Arms PH, **Symondsbury**
New Inn 🍴, **Stoke Abbott**
Pickwicks PH 🍴, Greyhound PH 🍴, lots of choice in **Beaminster**
Fox Inn 🍴, **Corscombe**
Talbot Inn, **Benville**
Swan Inn, **Toller Porcorum**
Three Horseshoes PH 🍴🍴, **Powerstock**

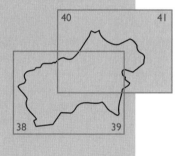

Benville   Uphall   Rampisham   Toller Porcorum   Bradford Peverell   Eggardon Hill   Powerstock   West Milton   Mangerton   Bradpole

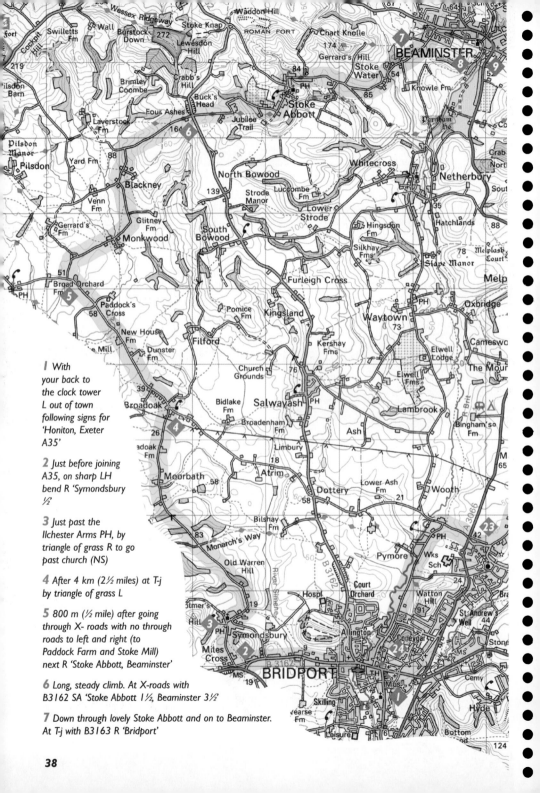

1 With your back to the clock tower L out of town following signs for 'Honiton, Exeter A35'

2 Just before joining A35, on sharp LH bend R 'Symondsbury ½'

3 Just past the Ilchester Arms PH, by triangle of grass R to go past church (NS)

4 After 4 km (2½ miles) at T-j by triangle of grass L

5 800 m (½ mile) after going through X- roads with no through roads to left and right (to Paddock Farm and Stoke Mill) next R 'Stoke Abbott, Beaminster'

6 Long, steady climb. At X-roads with B3162 SA 'Stoke Abbott 1½, Beaminster 3½'

7 Down through lovely Stoke Abbott and on to Beaminster. At T-j with B3163 R 'Bridport'

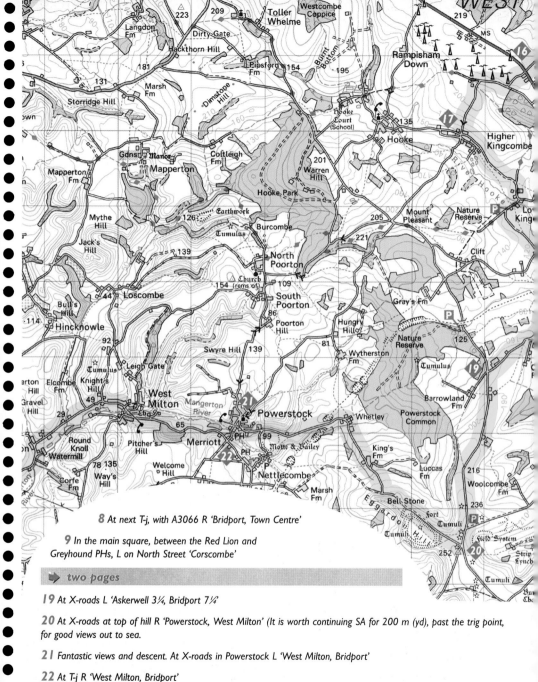

8 At next T-j, with A3066 R 'Bridport, Town Centre'

9 In the main square, between the Red Lion and
Greyhound PHs, L on North Street 'Corscombe'

➡ *two pages*

19 At X-roads L 'Askerwell 3¼, Bridport 7¼'

20 At X-roads at top of hill R 'Powerstock, West Milton' (It is worth continuing SA for 200 m (yd), past the trig point, for good views out to sea.

21 Fantastic views and descent. At X-roads in Powerstock L 'West Milton, Bridport'

22 At T-j R 'West Milton, Bridport'

23 Follow signs for Bridport. At X-roads with A356 SA 'Pymore ¼, Dottery 1½, then 1st L 'Bridport, Pyemore'

24 At T-j in Bridport L to return to clock tower

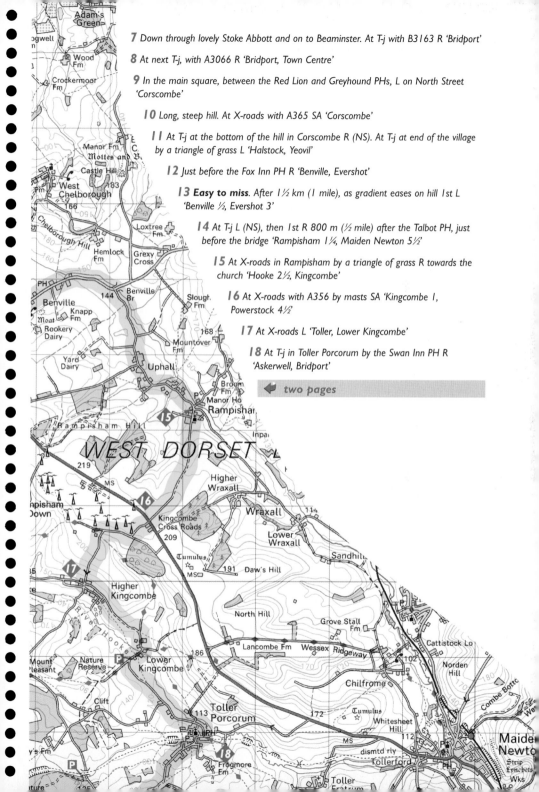

7 Down through lovely Stoke Abbott and on to Beaminster. At T-j with B3163 R 'Bridport'

8 At next T-j, with A3066 R 'Bridport, Town Centre'

9 In the main square, between the Red Lion and Greyhound PHs, L on North Street 'Corscombe'

10 Long, steep hill. At X-roads with A365 SA 'Corscombe'

11 At T-j at the bottom of the hill in Corscombe R (NS). At T-j at end of the village by a triangle of grass L 'Halstock, Yeovil'

12 Just before the Fox Inn PH R 'Benville, Evershot'

13 **Easy to miss**. After 1½ km (1 mile), as gradient eases on hill 1st L 'Benville ½, Evershot 3'

14 At T-j L (NS), then 1st R 800 m (½ mile) after the Talbot PH, just before the bridge 'Rampisham 1¼, Maiden Newton 5½'

15 At X-roads in Rampisham by a triangle of grass R towards the church 'Hooke 2½, Kingcombe'

16 At X-roads with A356 by masts SA 'Kingcombe 1, Powerstock 4½'

17 At X-roads L 'Toller, Lower Kingcombe'

18 At T-j in Toller Porcorum by the Swan Inn PH R 'Askerwell, Bridport'

◀ two pages

Valleys and downland west of Wilton

*T*hree river valleys (the Wylye, the Nadder and the Ebble) run almost parallel to the west of Wilton. This ride heads out along the valley formed by the River Wylye, passing several beautiful thatched houses in the villages of Great Wishford and Hanging Langford before turning south and crossing two downland ridges with fine views to reach the Ebble Valley at Fifield Bavant. The route now goes east to Bishopstone and recrosses the final ridge to return to Wilton.

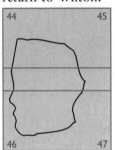

Start

The Square, Wilton

P On side streets or on roads out of town

Distance and grade

40 km (25 miles)

🚴🚴 Easy/moderate

Terrain

Two stretches of very gentle valley cycling linked by four climbs, the first, of 120 m (400 ft), south from Wylye; the second, of 61 m (200 ft), between Dinton and Fovant; the third (the steepest), of 91 m (300 ft), south of Fovant; and the final one, of 100 m (330 ft), north from Bishopstone

Nearest railway

Salisbury, 5 km (3 miles) from Wilton

Wilton

Great Wishford

Hanging Langford

Wylye

Dinton

Places of interest

Wilton 1

The word Wiltshire is derived from Wilton-shire. Wilton was King Egbert's capital and the foundations of the Royal Palace are thought to lie beneath the Georgian Houses in Kingsbury Square. For many centuries, Wilton has been best known for its carpet-making, and the Royal Wilton Carpet Factory is famous throughout the world.

Refreshments

Queens Head PH 🍴, **Broad Chalke**
Penruddock Arms PH, **Dinton**
The Bell PH 🍴🍴, **Wylye**
Royal Oak PH 🍴, **Great Wishford**
Wiltons PH 🍴, *plenty of choice in*
Wilton

Wilton House 1

Close to the start of the route. Wilton House stands on the site of a Saxon abbey that was given to William Herbert (later the 1st Earl of Pembroke) by Henry VIII. The original Tudor house and its contents were almost completely destroyed in a fire in about 1647. Rebuilding started immediately under the supervision of Inigo Jones and was completed in about 1653. The house is famous for its 'double cube' room and Palladian bridge. Its treasures include family portraits painted for the 4th Earl by Van Dyck, as well as paintings by Reynolds, Rembrandt, Rubens and Poussin and furniture by Chippendale and William Kent.

Philipps House, Dinton 5

A National Trust property lying to the west of the route designed by Jeffrey Wyattville and completed in 1816.

Fovant

Broad Chalke

Stoke Farthing

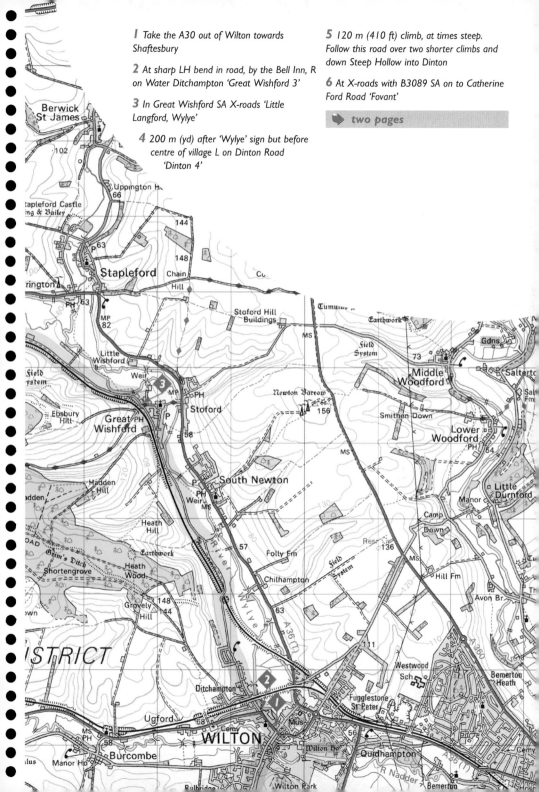

1 Take the A30 out of Wilton towards Shaftesbury

2 At sharp LH bend in road, by the Bell Inn, R on Water Ditchampton 'Great Wishford 3'

3 In Great Wishford SA X-roads 'Little Langford, Wylye'

4 200 m (yd) after 'Wylye' sign but before centre of village L on Dinton Road 'Dinton 4'

5 120 m (410 ft) climb, at times steep. Follow this road over two shorter climbs and down Steep Hollow into Dinton

6 At X-roads with B3089 SA on to Catherine Ford Road 'Fovant'

two pages

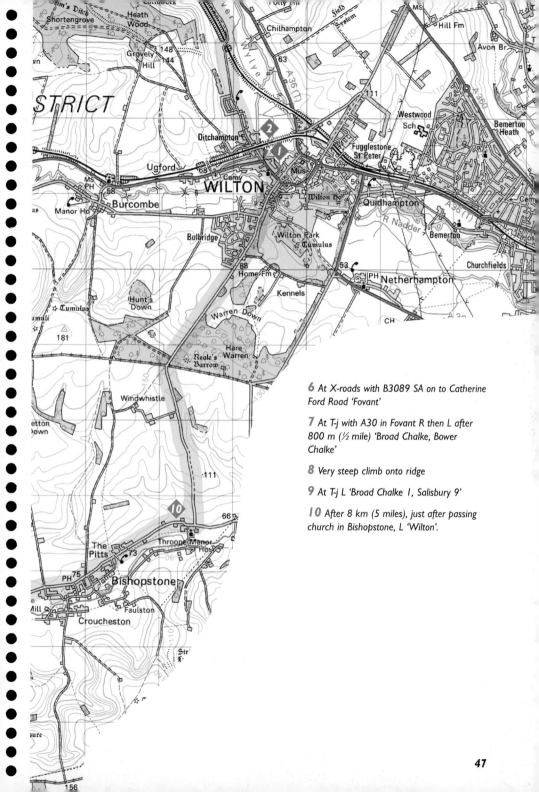

6 At X-roads with B3089 SA on to Catherine Ford Road 'Fovant'

7 At T-j with A30 in Fovant R then L after 800 m (½ mile) 'Broad Chalke, Bower Chalke'

8 Very steep climb onto ridge

9 At T-j L 'Broad Chalke 1, Salisbury 9'

10 After 8 km (5 miles), just after passing church in Bishopstone, L 'Wilton'.

The Somerset Levels south of Wedmore

Together with the Severn Vale, the Somerset Levels offer flat lands. However, flat does not mean boring, as the moors and levels are among the last remaining wetlands in the country and support a wide variety of wildlife. Huge mounds of rich dark peat and a network of drainage channels make this a most unusual landscape to cycle through. The ride also takes you through the mystical, magical town of Glastonbury, famous for its abbey and tor. As with all flat areas, very slight climbs can give fine viewpoints, and the climb onto the ridge southeast of Wedmore gives magnificent views not only of the Levels but also of the Mendips to the north.

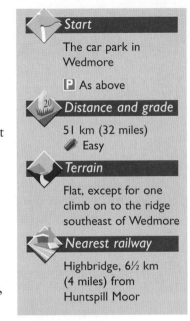

Start

The car park in Wedmore

P As above

Distance and grade

51 km (32 miles)

Easy

Terrain

Flat, except for one climb on to the ridge southeast of Wedmore

Nearest railway

Highbridge, 6½ km (4 miles) from Huntspill Moor

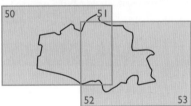

Wedmore

Cossington

Catcott

Shapwick

The Peat Moors Visitor Centre

This is situated at the Willows Garden Centre, a 3 km (2 mile) detour left at Shapwick crossroads (instruction 7). The centre illustrates the life, history, archaeology and natural history of the Somerset Levels. Tea rooms are also located at the garden centre.

Glastonbury ll

The ruined abbey at Glastonbury is on the site of the earliest Christian church of England and the body of King Arthur is reputed to be buried beneath the high altar. The ruins today consist mainly of the abbey church, St Mary's Chapel and various monastic buildings. In the gatehouse, there is a model of the abbey as it was in 1539. The Tor dominating the town in the east provides spectacular views and is crowned by the remaining tower of 15th-century St Michael's Chapel.

Somerset Rural Life Museum, Glastonbury ll

Set in what was once the principal tithe barn of the abbey, it has a late Victorian farmhouse, an exhibition of Cheddar cheese making and other displays of agriculture and Somerset industries. Various outdoor demonstrations and activities are held in the courtyard.

Refreshments

George PH 🍷, *plenty of choice in* **Wedmore**
King William PH 🍷, **Catcott**
Ashcott Inn 🍷🍷, **Ashcott**
Plenty of choice in **Glastonbury**
Panborough PH 🍷, **Panborough**

Glastonbury

Godney

Theale

Sand

1 Out of Wedmore on the B3139 towards Burnham. After 800 m (½ mile), at the edge of Wedmore, just past Wedmore First School on the right next L (NS)

2 Through Heath House down onto moor. At T-j with broad stone track ahead R (NS)

3 After 2½ km (1½ miles) 1st L between rows of pollarded willow trees (NS). After 800 m (½ mile) 1st L

4 After 2 km (1¼ miles), L at T-j 'Edington, Bridgwater', then 1st R 'Huntspill, Bridgwater'

5 At sharp RH bend L 'Gold Corner ¾, Cossington 3'

6 At T-j in Cossington L on Middle Road. Follow for 5½ km (3½ miles) through Chilton Polden, bypassing Catcott, turning L at X-roads 2 km (1¼ miles) past Catcott on Church Lane 'Shapwick ½, Westhay 3½'

7 At X-roads in Shapwick, SA onto Northbrook Road 'Ashcott 1½, Glastonbury 6¾'. After almost 800 m (½ mile) just before '7.5 Ton Weight Limit' sign 1st R

➡ **three pages**

17 1st R in Sand 'Wedmore ¾, Cheddar 4¾'. At T-j R 'Shapwick, Glastonbury'. At mini-roundabout SA onto Grants Lane to return to star

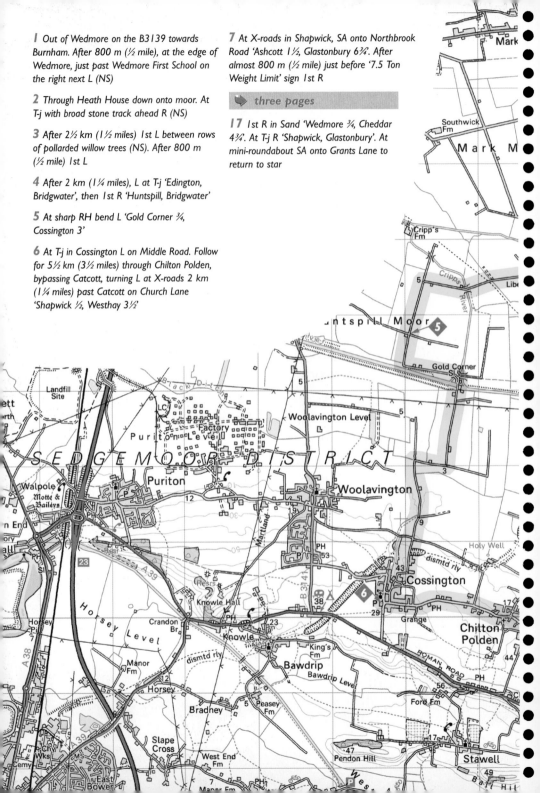

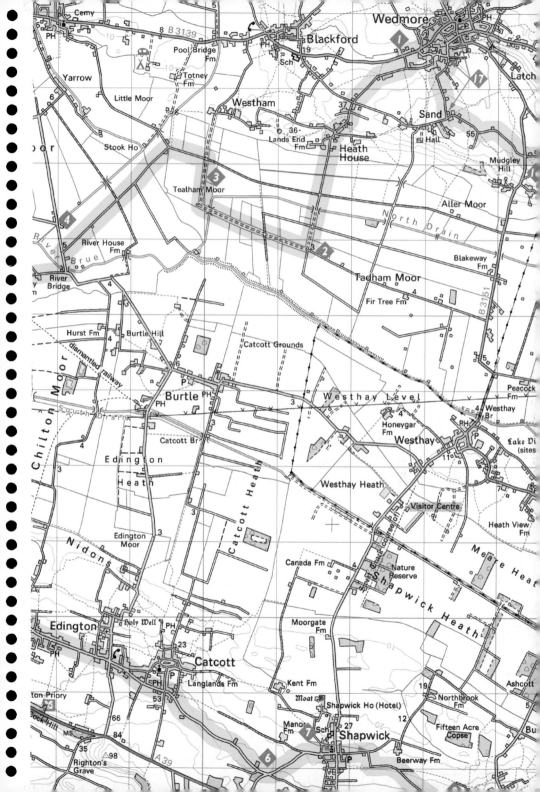

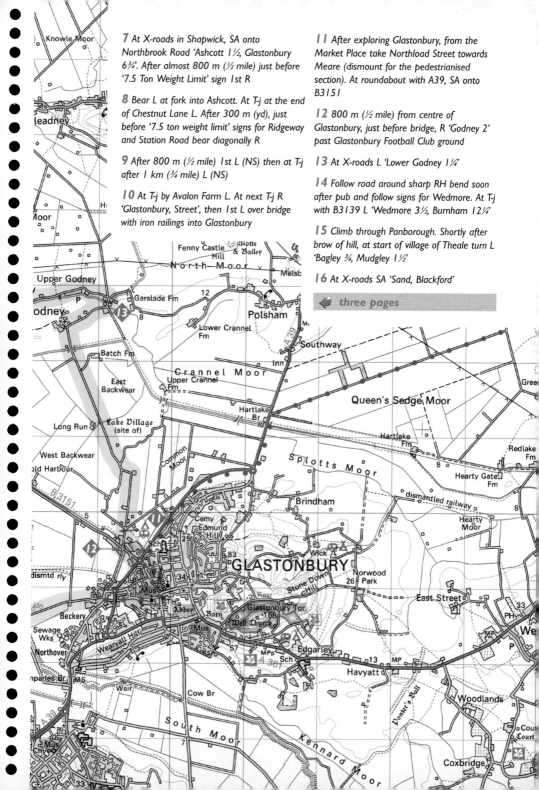

7 At X-roads in Shapwick, SA onto Northbrook Road 'Ashcott 1½, Glastonbury 6¾'. After almost 800 m (½ mile) just before '7.5 Ton Weight Limit' sign 1st R

8 Bear L at fork into Ashcott. At T-j at the end of Chestnut Lane L. After 300 m (yd), just before '7.5 ton weight limit' signs for Ridgeway and Station Road bear diagonally R

9 After 800 m (½ mile) 1st L (NS) then at T-j after 1 km (¾ mile) L (NS)

10 At T-j by Avalon Farm L. At next T-j R 'Glastonbury, Street', then 1st L over bridge with iron railings into Glastonbury

11 After exploring Glastonbury, from the Market Place take Northload Street towards Meare (dismount for the pedestrianised section). At roundabout with A39, SA onto B3151

12 800 m (½ mile) from centre of Glastonbury, just before bridge, R 'Godney 2' past Glastonbury Football Club ground

13 At X-roads L 'Lower Godney 1¼'

14 Follow road around sharp RH bend soon after pub and follow signs for Wedmore. At T-j with B3139 L 'Wedmore 3½, Burnham 12¼'

15 Climb through Panborough. Shortly after brow of hill, at start of village of Theale turn L 'Bagley ¾, Mudgley 1½'

16 At X-roads SA 'Sand, Blackford'

three pages

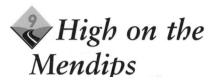

High on the Mendips

The Mendips are an outcrop of Carboniferous limestone stretching from Weston-super-Mare to Shepton Mallet, their most famous feature being the caves at Cheddar. The scenery is at times more reminiscent of the Yorkshire dales than southwest England, with squat grey stone houses and drystone walling. The best views are to be found by making two detours from the main route, each of 400 m (½ mile), to the radio masts near Charterhouse and to the edge of the steep southern slopes west of Priddy. The ride skirts the steep hills of the western end of the range and climbs via Winscombe and Shipham to its highest point 260 m (870 ft) near Tynings Farm. It continues along the top of the ridge to Chewton Mendip, then brings you back via the towering cliffs of Cheddar Gorge, the tourist complex of Cheddar and the quieter pleasures of Axbridge.

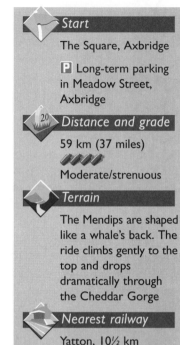

Start

The Square, Axbridge

P Long-term parking in Meadow Street, Axbridge

Distance and grade

59 km (37 miles)

Moderate/strenuous

Terrain

The Mendips are shaped like a whale's back. The ride climbs gently to the top and drops dramatically through the Cheddar Gorge

Nearest railway

Yatton, 10½ km (6½ miles) from Shipham

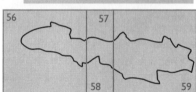

Axbridge   Winscombe   Star   Shipham   Charterhouse

Places of interest

King John's Hunting Lodge, Axbridge 2

An early 15th-century merchant's timber-framed house that has been extensively restored and converted into a museum of local history and archaeology. It has no apparent connection with King John, or with hunting, but was used as an ale house in the 17th- and 18th-centuries.

Lillypool Cider and Cheese Farm, Shipham 11

The farm dates back to the 18th-century and houses an exhibition of farming equipment and cider mills. There is a café, children's play area and nature trail, and local cider, cheese, homemade pickles and chutneys are for sale.

Chewton Cheese Dairy, Priory Farm, Chewton Mendip 21

One of the few dairies left making traditional Cheddar cheese from Fresian and Ayrshire herds. Morning coffee, farmhouse lunches and cream teas.

Cheddar Showcaves 29

These spectacular caves within the limestone gorge are an attraction of outstanding natural beauty. There are magnificent crystalline formations that have taken over half a million years to form. The Cheddar Caves Museum displays various archeological finds.

Refreshments

Lamb PH 🍺, plenty of choice in **Axbridge**
Waldegrave Arms PH 🍺, **East Harptree**
Hunters Lodge Inn 🍺, New Inn 🍺,
Queen Victoria Inn 🍺, **Priddy**
Tea shop at Cheese Farm, **Chewton Mendip**
Plenty of choice in **Cheddar**
Waldegrave Arms PH 🍺, **East Harptree**

East Harptree Litton Chewton Mendip Priddy Cheddar

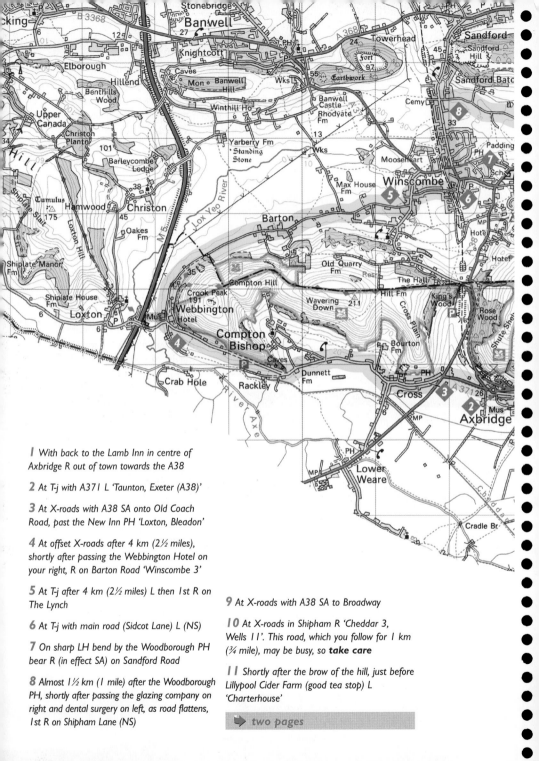

1 With back to the Lamb Inn in centre of Axbridge R out of town towards the A38

2 At T-j with A371 L 'Taunton, Exeter (A38)'

3 At X-roads with A38 SA onto Old Coach Road, past the New Inn PH 'Loxton, Bleadon'

4 At offset X-roads after 4 km (2½ miles), shortly after passing the Webbington Hotel on your right, R on Barton Road 'Winscombe 3'

5 At T-j after 4 km (2½ miles) L then 1st R on The Lynch

6 At T-j with main road (Sidcot Lane) L (NS)

7 On sharp LH bend by the Woodborough PH bear R (in effect SA) on Sandford Road

8 Almost 1½ km (1 mile) after the Woodborough PH, shortly after passing the glazing company on right and dental surgery on left, as road flattens, 1st R on Shipham Lane (NS)

9 At X-roads with A38 SA to Broadway

10 At X-roads in Shipham R 'Cheddar 3, Wells 11'. This road, which you follow for 1 km (¾ mile), may be busy, so **take care**

11 Shortly after the brow of the hill, just before Lillypool Cider Farm (good tea stop) L 'Charterhouse'

➡ two pages

29 *Through Cheddar Gorge and Cheddar. Opposite the Butchers Arms PH on your left R on Tweentown 'Weston-super-Mare' (A371)*

30 *After 800 m (½ mile), opposite the Catholic church, L on Lower North Street 'Baptist Church'*

31 *At T-j with A371, opposite shop, R then shortly L on Station Road, 'B3151 Wedmore'*

32 *2nd R, into Valley Line Industrial Estate, then on to Axbridge Cycleway*

33 *At end of cycleway, at T-j with main road L then L again 'Axbridge'*

12 Steady then steep climb to the plateau. After 5½ km (3½ miles), L at X-roads 'Burrington 3½, Blagdon 2¼ (After 400 m (yd), 1st L to radio masts for fine views or on to trig point for even better ones!). **For short cut** turn R at the X-roads 'Priddy 3½, Cheddar 5½ and follow signs for Cheddar
back to the start

13 At T-j with B3134 R 'Cheddar 7½'

14 After 1½ km (1 mile), at truck repair yard L 'Compton Martin, West Harptree'

15 Go straight across two X-roads. **Take care** down steep hill!

16 At 3rd X-roads, with Mead Cottage ahead and a sign for 'Western Lane' near your right pedal (!), L

17 At the end of Middle Street, at T-j by the stores in East Harptree, R

18 After 1 km (¾ mile) at T-j beneath telephone wires R (NS)

19 On sharp RH bend L 'Litton 1¼, Chewton Mendip 1'

20 At T-j with B3114 R 'Chewton Mendip ½, Wells 6¼'

21 At X-roads with A39 SA then 1st R on Bray's Batch, bearing L at fork. You are now on Puppy Lane

22 At X-roads R (NS). At X-roads with A39 SA 'Cheddar 9¾, Burrington 9½ (1st R to Priory Farm for an excellent tea stop)

23 At T-j with B3135 R 'Priddy, Cheddar, Burrington'

24 At X-roads by Miners Arms PH L 'Priddy, Milton'

25 At X-roads by Hunters Lodge Inn R 'Priddy 1½, Cheddar 7'

26 In Priddy L at New Inn PH

27 After 1½ km (1 mile), at T-j R (NS) (detour L for 800 m (½ mile) for fine views to the south)

28 At T-j with B3135 L 'Cheddar 5'

two pages

Over the Brendon Hills, east of Dulverton

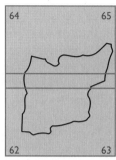

The two major climbs in this ride are well worth the effort for the superb views from the Brendon Hills. The first climb starts at the ford at Bury, east of Dulverton, and swiftly reaches the top of Haddon Hill, where the view opens out. More gentle climbing takes you to the first high point of 400 m (1300 ft) at the masts near Brendon Hill Farm. A 6½ km (4 mile) descent, which provides occasional views of the sea, drops you at the Washford River in Hungerford. From here a lovely riverside climb 350 m (1150 ft) brings you onto the second 400 m (1300 ft) high point. An undulating ridge ride drops steeply at the end to return to Dulverton.

 Start

The Lion Hotel, Dulverton

P Follow signs in Dulverton

 Distance and grade

54 km (34 miles)

Strenuous

Terrain

Steep 190 m (630 ft) climb from Bury onto Haddon Hill. 160 m (530 ft) climb from Upton to the masts at the top of the hill. 400 m (1200 ft) climb over 14 km (9 miles) from Washford to Lype Hill

 Nearest railway

Washford, 1½ km (1 mile) from Hungerford

 Refreshments

Plenty of choice in **Dulverton**
Ralegh's Cross Inn 🍴🍴, **Ralegh's Cross**
Royal Oak PH 🍴🍴, **Luxborough**
Valiant Soldier PH, **Roadwater**

Dulverton

Bury

Haddon Hill

Upton

Sticklepath

Hungerford

West Somerset Railway

This is Britain's longest independent railway. It runs from Bishop's Lydeard near Taunton to Minehead passing about 800 m (½ mile) from the route at Washford. Many of the trains are steam-hauled.

Cleeve Abbey, Washford 7

Cleeve Abbey was founded by the Earl of Lincoln in 1198 and is the only Cistercian abbey in Somerset. It has been well renovated and the remaining buidings include the refectory, chapter house, common-room and the cloisters.

▲ Exmoor

Roadwater

Luxborough

Couple Cross

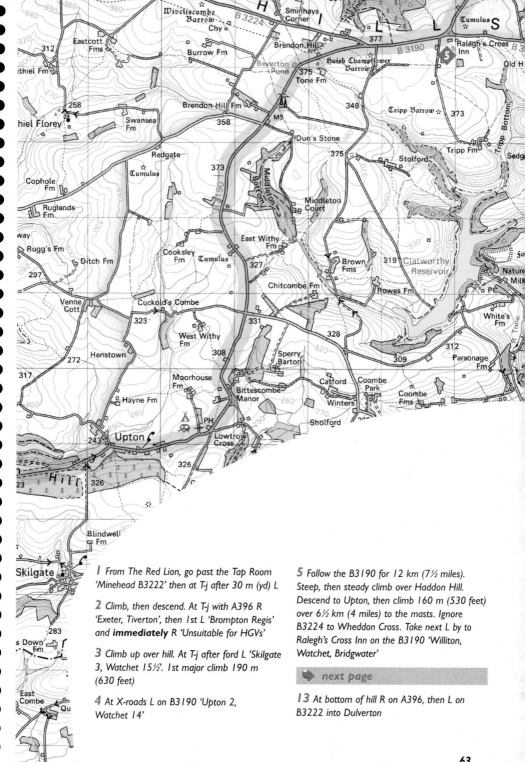

1 From The Red Lion, go past the Tap Room 'Minehead B3222' then at T-j after 30 m (yd) L

2 Climb, then descend. At T-j with A396 R 'Exeter, Tiverton', then 1st L 'Brompton Regis' and **immediately** R 'Unsuitable for HGVs'

3 Climb up over hill. At T-j after ford L 'Skilgate 3, Watchet 15½'. 1st major climb 190 m (630 feet)

4 At X-roads L on B3190 'Upton 2, Watchet 14'

5 Follow the B3190 for 12 km (7½ miles). Steep, then steady climb over Haddon Hill. Descend to Upton, then climb 160 m (530 feet) over 6½ km (4 miles) to the masts. Ignore B3224 to Wheddon Cross. Take next L by to Ralegh's Cross Inn on the B3190 'Williton, Watchet, Bridgwater'

➡ *next page*

13 At bottom of hill R on A396, then L on B3222 into Dulverton

5 Follow the B3190 for 12 km (7½ miles). Steep, then steady climb over Haddon Hill. Descend to Upton, then climb 160 m (530 ft) over 6½ km (4 miles) to the masts. Ignore B3224 to Wheddon Cross. Take next L by to Ralegh's Cross Inn on the B3190 'Williton, Watchet, Bridgwater'

6 Fast descent, short climb, 2nd fast descent. At X-roads after almost 6½ km (4 miles) by large red sandstone house and signpost with myriad Somerset names L 'Washford 1¾, Minehead 7¾'

7 At White Horse Inn in Hungerford L 'Roadwater 1½, Treborough 3½, Luxborough 5¾'. Start of 2nd climb 400 m (1200 ft) over 14 km (9 miles)

8 At the far end of Roadwater, 400 m (yd) after the Valiant Soldier PH R 'Luxborough 3¾'

9 In Luxborough, ignore 1st R near Inn but take 2nd R, after crossing bridge 'Dunster 5½'

10 Steep climb to Churchtown. At T-j by Butchers Farm bear L (in effect SA) then after further 800 m (½ mile) climb by triangle of grass with trees and bench L 'Timberscombe 3¾, Wheddon Cross 4½'

11 At X-roads L 'Wheddon Cross 3, Dulverton 9'

12 At X-roads SA 'Brompton Regis 4¼, Dulverton 7½'

◀ previous page

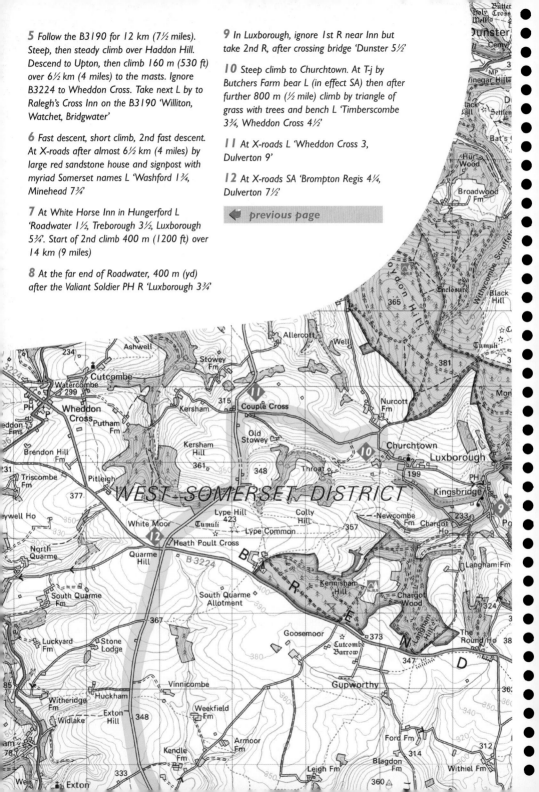

Take care not to mistake the faded yellow line of the national park boundary for the solid yellow line of the route.

The roof of Exmoor, west of Dulverton

Dulverton is a beautiful place set in the valley of the Barle, but if you like cycling away from main roads, there are no real alternatives to some very steep climbs. The climb onto the moor is very hard, so don't feel disheartened if you have to walk; it is only a mile and gives you access to a magnificent ridge ride on the very roof of Exmoor. The Sportsman's Inn at Sandyway Cross is about as unlikely a location for a pub as you will ever find and a welcome stopping-off point before the second major climb (much more gradual this time, 91 m (300 ft) in 3 km (2 miles) up to the high point of the ride 500 m (1600 ft) near Kinsford Gate. It is time to strap everything down and make doubly sure that your brakes work for the descent into Simonsbath and for a choice of refreshment stops. The final climb is to the top of Winsford Hill and the long descent through woodland by the River Barle to return to Dulverton.

70   71

68   69

Start

The Lion Hotel, Dulverton

P Follow signs in centre of Dulverton

Distance and grade

51 km (32 miles)

Strenuous

Terrain

350 m (1150 ft) climb from Dulverton to the highpoint at Hangley Cleave divided into three sections: very steep 170 m (550 ft) climb out of Dulverton, gentle 91 m (300 ft) climb across Anstey and Molland Common, steady 91 m (300 ft) climb from Sportsman's Inn to the top. 100 m (330 ft) climb out of Simonsbath. 70 m (230 ft) climb from Comer's Cross to Winsford Hill

Nearest railway

Tiverton Parkway, 29 km (18 miles) from Dulverton

Dulverton

Molland Common

Kinsford Gate

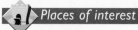
Places of interest

Dulverton

Named 'The Secret Place' by Saxon settlers, Dulverton has a special unspoilt charm with narrow lanes and cobbled alleys. The Guildhall Centre in the middle of Dulverton has exhibitions of all kinds throughout the year. At Exmoor House beside the River Barle, there are the headquarters of the National Park Authority and Dulverton Art Gallery.

Refreshments

Plenty of choice in
Dulverton
Sportsman's Inn,
Sandyway Cross
Simonsbath Hotel,
Simonsbath

▲ *Exmoor*

Simonsbath   White Cross   Comer's Cross   Winsford Hill

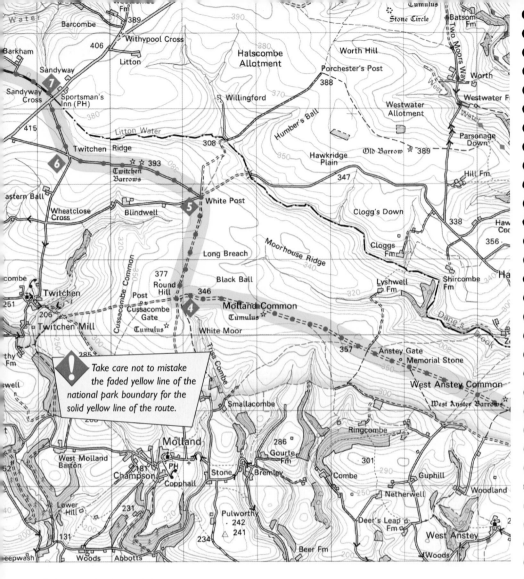

Take care not to mistake the faded yellow line of the national park boundary for the solid yellow line of the route.

1 Take the B3223 towards Lynton

2 After 1½ km (1 mile) L 'Hawkridge 4'. 1st climb 150 m (500 ft)

3 At Five Ways Cross SA 'Molland 6'

4 After 8 km (5 miles) along this magnificent ridge, at X-roads at Ridgeway Cross R 'Hawkridge 4, Withypool 6'

5 After 1½ km (1 mile) at White Post Cross L over cattle grid and immediately bear R uphill

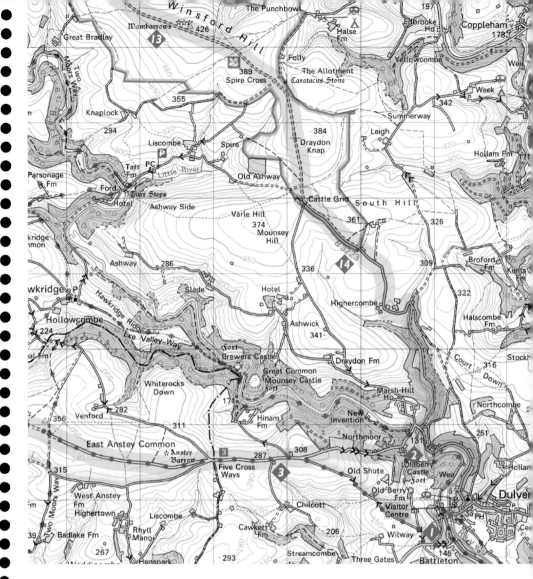

6 At Mudgate Cross R 'Sandyway, Withypool'

7 At Sandyway Cross R then L, following signs for Simonsbath or stop at the pub here

 next page

13 4th climb 70 m (230 ft) to Winsford Hill

14 Final descent 140 m (465 ft) to Dulverton

8 2nd climb 91 m (300 ft) to highest point of ride

9 At Kinsford Gate Cross R 'Simonsbath, Lynton'

10 Steep drop to Simonsbath and choice of restaurant or pub

11 At T-j in Simonsbath R on B3223 'Exford, Minehead', – 3rd climb 70 m (230 ft)

12 This section may be busy. After 8 km (5 miles) R on B3223 'Withypool 2½, Dulverton 10'

13 4th climb 70 m (230 ft) to Winsford Hill

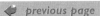 previous page

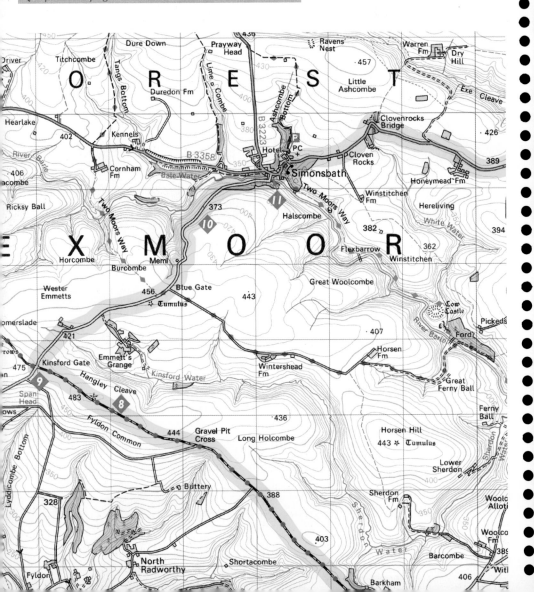

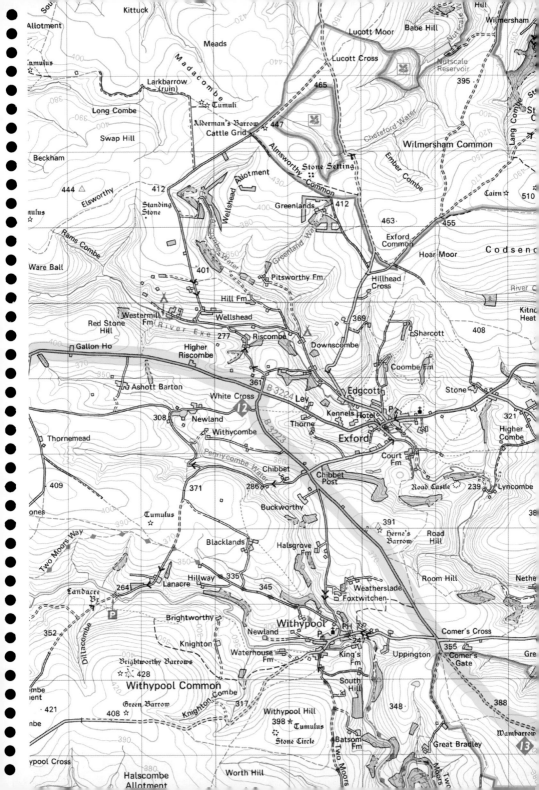

From the hills to the Levels northeast of Ilminster

East from Ilminster the ride passes through some amazing cuttings near Dinnington, then through the beautiful village of Hinton St George. The one steep climb of the route takes you to the top of Ham

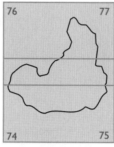

Hill, where the views are more than an adequate reward. A steep drop through Stoke Sub Hamdon leads on to Martock and the moors of southern Somerset. The abbey at Muchelney is well worth a visit simply for its incongruous setting in the middle of the Somerset wetlands. The ride passes more lovely houses and deep cuttings on the return via Kingsbury Episcopi and Shepton Beauchamp to Ilminster.

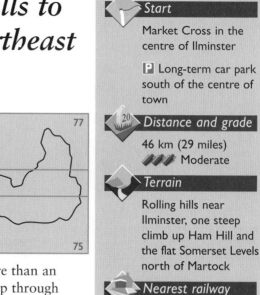

Start

Market Cross in the centre of Ilminster

P Long-term car park south of the centre of town

Distance and grade

46 km (29 miles)
Moderate

Terrain

Rolling hills near Ilminster, one steep climb up Ham Hill and the flat Somerset Levels north of Martock

Nearest railway

Crewkerne 5½ km (3½ miles) from the route at Merriott

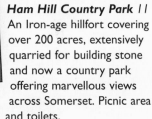

Hamstone Villages

Hinton St George, the Chinnocks, Chiselborough and Stoke Sub Hamdon. The belt of limestone that stretches across south Somerset changes colour and character, from Golden Hamstone in the North to Blue Lias in the South. This stone has been the main building material of past centuries, so the change in the landscape is reflected by the local villages.

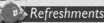

▲ Hinton St George

Ham Hill Country Park 11

An Iron-age hillfort covering over 200 acres, extensively quarried for building stone and now a country park offering marvellous views across Somerset. Picnic area and toilets.

Muchelney 15

Once the site of a great Benedictine abbey founded in AD 950. There is an excavated ground plan of the abbey and church and well-preserved remains of a 15th-century cloister and Abbot's lodgings.

Barrington Court Garden
between 17 and 18
Attractive 16th-century 'E'-shaped house restored in the early 20th-century. In the grounds, there is a beautiful, walled garden with a kitchen garden supplying produce for the Strode Restaurant that is open for hot and cold lunches and afternoon teas.

Refreshments

Plenty of choice in **Ilminster**
Poulett Arms PH 🍺🍺, **Hinton St George**
Cat Head Inn, **Chiselborough**
Prince of Wales PH, **Ham Hill**
Half Moon PH, Fleur de Lys PH,
Stoke Sub Hamdon
Plenty of choice in **Martock**
Wyndham Arms PH 🍺,
Kingsbury Episcopi
Royal Oak PH 🍺, **Barrington**

Muchelney

West Lambrook

Shepton Beauchamp

Barrington

1 From the Market Hall take East Street past the Post Office out of Ilminster

2 At T-j 'Seavington St. Michael, Ilchester'. Shortly, at White Horse PH 1st R 'Kingstone, Crewkerne, Dowlish'

3 **Ignore** two left turns in quick succession and also next left turn to Allowenshay. Shortly, on sharp RH bend turn L 'Dinnington. Unsuitable for HGVs'

4 At T-j bear L (NS) then shortly 2nd R 'Hinton St George 1½, Merriott 2¾'. Wonderful sunken lanes. At next T-j with letter box in wall opposite R (NS)

5 1½ km (1 mile) after Hinton St George, at T-j R 'Crewkerne' then 1st L onto Church Street 'Scotts Nurseries'

6 At T-j in Merriott L 'Martock, Ilchester'

7 At T-j with A356 R then 1st L 'West Chinnock, Middle Chinnock'

8 At T-j at the end of Scotts Way L onto Lower Street

9 Through West Chinnock. Ignore 1st turn right by triangle of grass to Middle Chinnock and follow signs for Chiselborough. Shortly after brow of hill and LH bend at the start of Chiselborough, turn R opposite bus shelter 'Norton, Ham Hill'

10 On sharp LH bend R (in effect SA) 'Little Norton, Ham Hill, Unsuitable for HGVs'. Steep climb, brilliant views

11 At T-j at top of hill L (NS). Picnic or stop for refreshment at Prince of Wales PH

12 Descend into Stoke Sub Hamdon. At T-j L then 1st R onto North Street 'Martock'

➡ *next page*

16 Follow this road for 10½ km (6½ miles) through Kingsbury into Shepton Beauchamp. At Duke of York PH

bear R (in effect SA) on Great Lane up an amazing road cut into the 'bowels of Somerset'

17 At X-roads R 'Barrington, Langport, Taunton'

18 At T-j with B3168 bear L 'Puckington, Ilminster' to return to Ilminster

11 *At T-j at top of hill L (NS). Picnic or stop for refreshment at Prince of Wales PH*

12 *Descend into Stoke Sub Hamdon. At T-j L then 1st R onto North Street 'Martock'*

13 *After 2½ km (1½ miles), at T-j with B3165, opposite Brooks Garage, R 'Martock'*

14 Easy to miss. *Through Martock. 2½ km (1½ miles) after the end of the village L 'Muchelney, Muchelney Abbey'*

15 *At T-j L 'Muchelney Pottery' (or R to visit Muchelney Abbey)*

16 *Follow this road for 10½ km (6½ miles) through Kingsbury into Shepton Beauchamp. At Duke of York PH bear R (in effect SA) on Great Lane up an amazing road cut into the 'bowels of Somerset'*

17 *At X-roads R 'Barrington, Langport, Taunton'*

18 *At T-j with B3168 bear L 'Puckington, Ilminster' to return to Ilminster*

⬅ previous page

From the Somerset Levels to the Blackdown Hills west of Ilminster

The first 16 km (10 miles) of the ride take you over the Levels of southern Somerset, where all the water drains into the River Isle, hence 'Ilminster', 'Ilton' and 'Isle Abbotts'. The lush pastures of the lowlands give way to the the wooded slopes of the Blackdown Hills. As far as Churchinford, the climbs are long and steady. On the return from Churchinford to Ilminster, there are three very sharp ascents but you are more than compensated for your effort by the fabulous views.

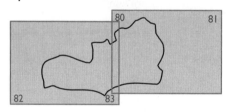

 Start

Market Cross in the centre of Ilminster

P Long-term car park south of the centre of town

 Distance and grade

51 km (32 miles)
Moderate/strenuous

 Terrain

From the flat Somerset Levels at 15 m (50 ft) to the Blackdown Hills at 300 m (1000 ft), this is a ride of contrasts

 Nearest railway

Taunton, 10 km (6 miles) from the route at Staple Fitzpaine or Crewkerne, 13 km (8 miles) from Ilminster

Ilminster   Isle Abbotts   Curry Mallet   Hatch Beauchamp   Staple Fitzpaine

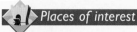

Places of interest

Ilminster /

The spectacular church of St Mary, with its perpendicular tower, stands in this market town. It is modelled on Wells Cathedral, and inside there is the family tomb of the Wadhams, founders of Wadham College in Oxford.

Refreshments

Plenty of choice in **Ilminster**
Greyhound Inn ❦, **Staple Fitzpaine**
The Bell Inn, **Curry Mallet**
Hatch Inn, **Hatch Beauchamp**
York Inn, **Churchstanton**
Candlelight Inn, **Bishopswood**

▲ Near Churchinford

Holman Glavel   Churchinford   Bishopswood   Sticklepath   Crock Street

1 Follow the one-way system west out of Ilminster 'Langport, Taunton'

2 After 150 m (yd), at T-j L, then 1st R onto B3168 'Curry Rivel, Langport'

3 800 m (½ mile) after crossing bridge over A303, on sharp RH bend, L 'Isle Abbotts, Ilton', then immediately R 'Isle Abbotts'

4 Follow the road right through Isle Abbotts, turning L at the church with its gargoyles

5 Shortly after church, at T-j bear R (in effect SA) then at next T-j R again

6 After 800 m (½ mile), at next T-j L 'Curry Mallet, Hatch Beauchamp'

7 After 300 m (yd) 1st R (NS). After 1 km (¾ mile), at T-j L (NS) into Curry Mallet

8 At T-j with Halfway House opposite R (NS). Go past Hatch Court into Hatch Beauchamp

9 With the Hatch Inn PH ahead, R then L onto the old A358 'Ilminster, Chard'

10 At the new A358 R then L 'Bickenhall, Staple Fitzpaine'

➡ **next page**

25 At offset X-roads R then L (NS)

26 At T-j with A358, look for small path slightly R of SA to gain access to track. Go SA where track joins road

27 At T-j bear L into Ilminster and return to start

9 With the Hatch Inn PH ahead, R then L onto the old A358 'Ilminster, Chard'

10 At the new A358 R then L 'Bickenhall, Staple Fitzpaine'

11 At T-j L 'Staple Fitzpaine 1½'

12 At X-roads L 'Combe St Nicholas, Chard'

13 Climb 140 m (450 ft) over 4 km (2½ miles). At T-j R 'Wellington, Honiton'

14 Climb further 61 m (200 ft) to high point of ride at 300 m (1000 ft)

15 At X-roads with B3170 SA 'Wellington, Churchinford'

16 After 400 m (¼ mile) 1st L 'Churchinford, Churchstanton'. At X-roads SA 'Bird Garden'

17 At T-j, with masts ahead, L 'Churchinford, Churchstanton'

18 At X-roads by the York Inn in the centre of Churchinford sharply L onto Royston Road 'Bishopswood 3, Ilminster 10'

19 1st of three short, steep climbs 61 m (200 ft)

20 At X-roads with B3170 SA 'Bishopswood, Chard'

21 Through Bishopswood. 2nd steep climb 79 m (260 ft)

22 At X-roads with A303, **extremely carefully,** SA 'Crickleaze, Whitestaunton'

23 3rd steep hill 54 m (180 ft) – the worst! At X-roads L (NS)

24 After 800 m (½ mile), on sharp LH bend, SA 'Sticklepath ½'. This is a difficult junction: go past it, cross over when you have clear views of the road in both directions, then return to junction

25 At offset X-roads R then L (NS)

← previous page

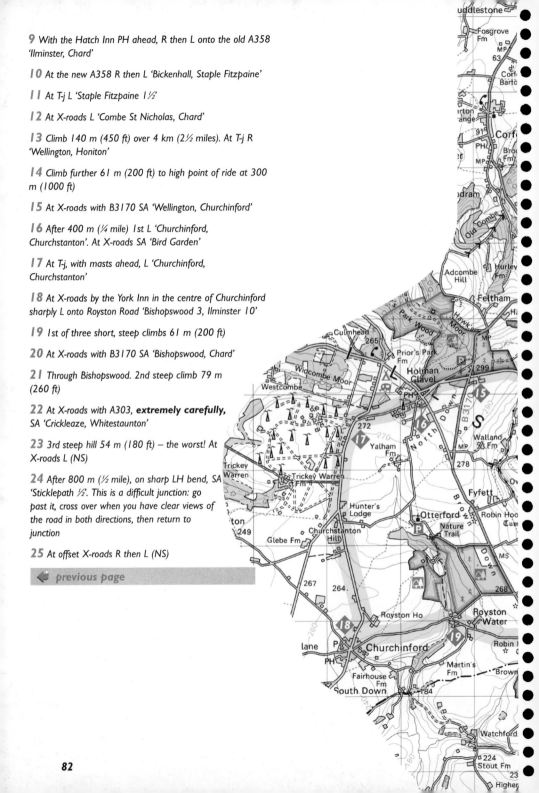

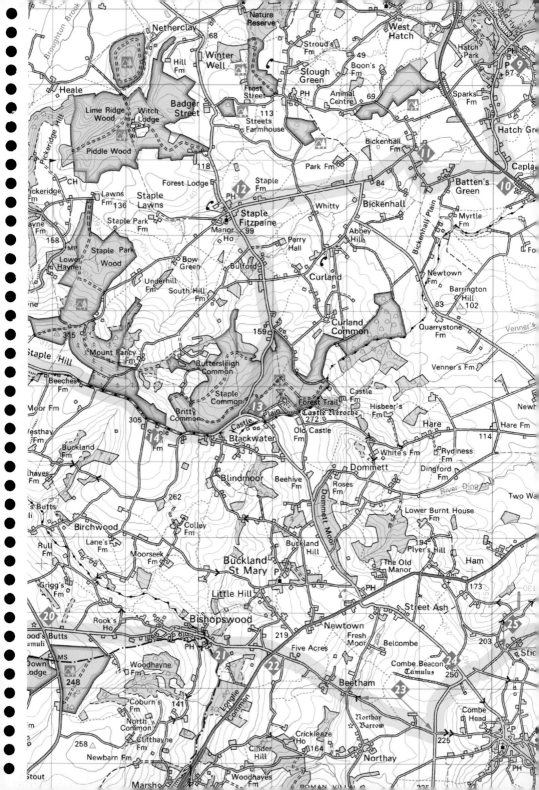

From Ottery St Mary to Exmouth and Budleigh, then back via the Otter valley

14

Start

The Volunteer Inn PH, Ottery St Mary

P Long-stay car park on road towards Talaton

Distance and grade

48 km (30 miles)

Easy/moderate

Terrain

Two main climbs: 91 m (300 ft) west from the Otter valley to Aylesbeare and 100 m (330 ft) from Exmouth to above Budleigh Salterton

Nearest railway

Exmouth

This is a reasonably easy ride. Ottery St Mary is a busy little town that stages one of the most extraordinary bonfire nights you are ever likely to come across: men charge around the narrow, crowded streets with burning barrels on their shoulders. The ride starts and finishes by following the quiet lane along the Otter valley between Ottery St Mary and Fluxton. The route climbs out of the valley and heads southwest through Aylesbeare and Woodbury down to the sea at Exmouth, with fine views west across the estuary. You have to climb inland before rejoining the sea at the more genteel resort of Budleigh Salterton. The final third of the ride follows the delightful valley of the River Otter north through Otterton and Tipton St John and back to Ottery St Mary.

86   87

88   89

Ottery St Mary   Metcombe   Aylesbeare   Nine Oaks   Woodbury   Exmouth

A La Ronde, north of Exmouth 14/15

This unique, 16-sided house was built in 1796 by Misses Jane and Mary Parminter. It combines the features of a rustic cottage with the style of the Basilica of Ravenna. Its rooms and Gothic grottoes are arranged around an octagonal hall.

Refreshments

Lots of choice in Ottery St Mary
Halfway PH ❤, *Aylesbeare Inn PH,* Aylesbeare
Diggers Rest PH ❤❤, Woodbury Salterton
Maltsters Arms PH, White Hart PH, Woodbury
Lots of choice in Exmouth
Salterton Arms PH ❤ *and others in* Budleigh Salterton
Kings Arms PH ❤, Otterton
Golden Lion PH ❤❤, Tipton St John

Exmouth 16/17

Situated on the estuary of the River Exe, this pleasant town and small port is the oldest and one of the largest seaside resorts in Devon. There are beautiful views west to Haldon and Dartmoor.

Budleigh Salterton 21

During the 13th-century, Budleigh Salterton was a salt-panning community supplying the local priory. There are several Georgian houses in the town and an art centre and museum at 27 Fore Street. Sir Walter Raleigh was born in a farmhouse nearby.

Otterton 24

Fine thatched cottages and a chestnut grove make this one of the most picturesque villages in the area. The restored Otterton Watermill is now a craft centre.

Bicton Park, near Otterton 24

Bicton Park comprises 50 acres of glorious gardens and parkland. There are glasshouses with fuchsias and geraniums and orchid houses.

Littleham   Budleigh Salterton   Otterton   Bridge End   Tipton St John

1 With back to Volunteer Inn PH L. At T-j with Canaan Way by St Anthony's Catholic Church L

2 Cross bridge and 1st L on Strawberry Way 'West Hill'. After 400 m (yd), at Salston Corner 1st L 'Fluxton 1½, Tipton St John 2'

3 Through Fluxton. Opposite telephone box by Angela Court Retirement Home R on Metcombe Vale 'Metcombe Vale ¼. West Hill 2¼, Aylesbeare 3'

4 At X-roads with B3180 at Tipton Cross SA 'Aylesbeare 1½'

5 At X-roads by Aylesbeare village hall, with white house ahead L 'Exmouth 8, Village Centre ¼'

6 1st R by Aylesbeare Inn PH onto Withen Lane 'Unsuitable for long vehicles'

7 At T-j at Withen Cross L. At X-roads with A3052 SA 'Unsuitable for long vehicles' **(Take care)**

8 After 800 m (½ mile) 1st R by triangle of grass

9 At T-j with breeze block barn ahead L (Brooklands Farm)

10 At T-j with Village Road L (in effect SA) 'Woodbury ¾'

11 In Woodbury, at X-roads with B3179 SA 'Lympstone 3, Exmouth 4'

⇨ *three pages*

25 Gradual climb for 1½ km (1 mile). On sharp RH bend 1st L 'Northmostown 1¾'

26 At T-j with busy A3052 R, then L on Higher Way 'Harpford ¼'**(Take care)**

27 At T-j in Tipton St John L 'Venn Ottery 1, West Hill 2¾' past the Golden Lion PH

28 At T-j with B3177 R 'Ottery St Mary ½'

29 At T-j with B3174 R into town centre. Follow one-way system, turning R onto Hind Street to return to start

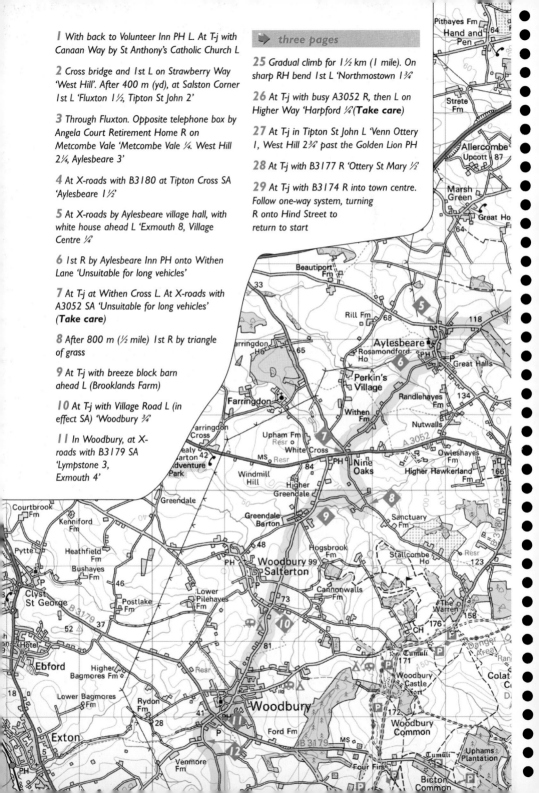

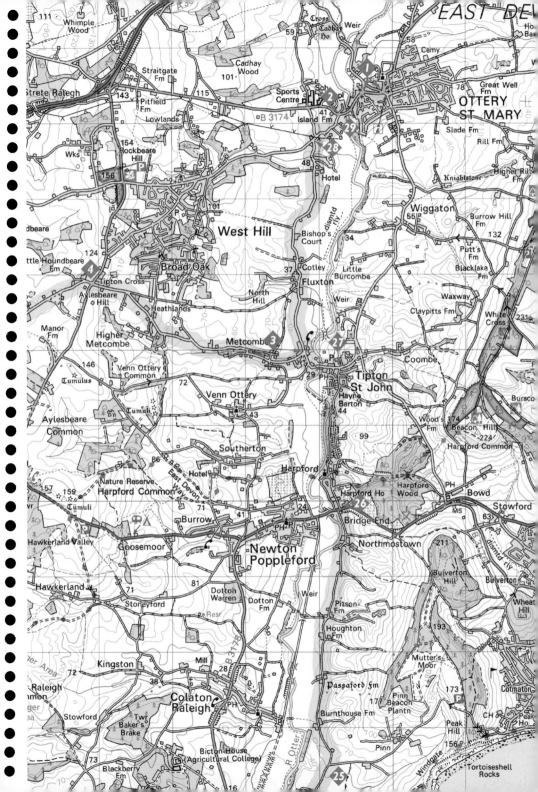

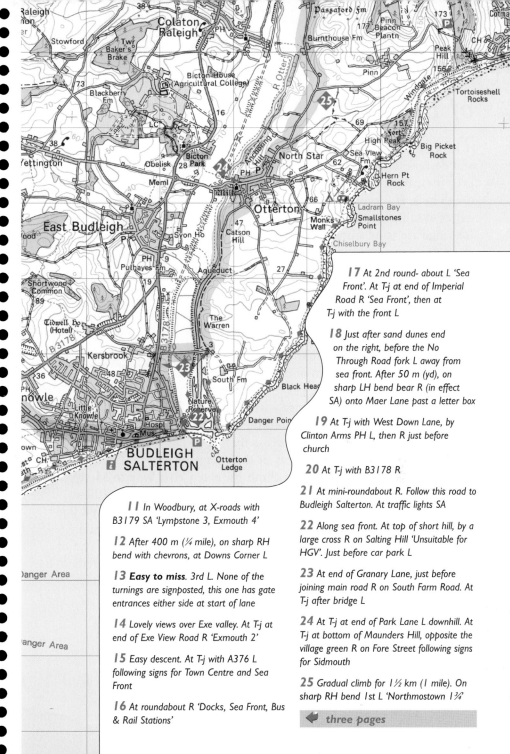

17 At 2nd round- about L 'Sea Front'. At T-j at end of Imperial Road R 'Sea Front', then at T-j with the front L

18 Just after sand dunes end on the right, before the No Through Road fork L away from sea front. After 50 m (yd), on sharp LH bend bear R (in effect SA) onto Maer Lane past a letter box

19 At T-j with West Down Lane, by Clinton Arms PH L, then R just before church

20 At T-j with B3178 R

21 At mini-roundabout R. Follow this road to Budleigh Salterton. At traffic lights SA

22 Along sea front. At top of short hill, by a large cross R on Salting Hill 'Unsuitable for HGV'. Just before car park L

23 At end of Granary Lane, just before joining main road R on South Farm Road. At T-j after bridge L

24 At T-j at end of Park Lane L downhill. At T-j at bottom of Maunders Hill, opposite the village green R on Fore Street following signs for Sidmouth

25 Gradual climb for 1½ km (1 mile). On sharp RH bend 1st L 'Northmostown 1¾'

11 In Woodbury, at X-roads with B3179 SA 'Lympstone 3, Exmouth 4'

12 After 400 m (¼ mile), on sharp RH bend with chevrons, at Downs Corner L

13 Easy to miss. 3rd L. None of the turnings are signposted, this one has gate entrances either side at start of lane

14 Lovely views over Exe valley. At T-j at end of Exe View Road R 'Exmouth 2'

15 Easy descent. At T-j with A376 L following signs for Town Centre and Sea Front

16 At roundabout R 'Docks, Sea Front, Bus & Rail Stations'

◀ **three pages**

From South Molton to the roof of Exmoor

This ride features a reasonably good ridge and descent. Needless to say, you have to earn these delights by climbing two long, tough hills. It is worth waiting for a clear day to do this ride as the views from along the ridge are truly stupendous. The ride starts from the unspoilt, unpretentious town of South Molton, the focal point for south west Exmoor. It then heads west, parallel with the busy North Devon link road, as far as Yarnacott. The first big hill, with a particularly savage start near Yarnacott, climbs 183 m (600 ft) to Kimbland Cross, above Brayford. Ahead of you, lies the next challenge – a descent into the valley to cross the River Bray at the village of Brayford and a 366 m (1200 ft) climb via Five Cross Way to Mole's Chamber. The next 16 km (10 miles), 10 km (6 miles) across the roof of Exmoor, then 6 km (4 miles) down to North Molton, must rate amongst the very finest in the country; there's even a pub at the end of the ridge and before the downhill. An unexpected short climb needs to be tackled to pass through North Molton on the way back to the start.

Start

The Clocktower, South Molton

P Long-stay car park south of the High Street

Distance and grade

48 km (30 miles)

///// Strenuous

Terrain

Two climbs: 183 m (600 ft) north from Yarnacott to Stone Cross and 366 m (1200 ft) from Brayford to Hangley Cleave on top of Exmoor

Nearest railway

Barnstaple, 8 km (5 miles) west of Yarnacott

94 | 95

92 | 93

South Molton — Shallowford — Riverton — Yarnacott — Stone Cross — Brayford — Five Cross Way

South Molton 1

Between the Middle Ages and the mid-19th-century, South Molton became a thriving wool town. It was also a coach stop

▼ Exmoor

on the route to Barnstaple and Bideford, and the nearest town to the iron and copper mines of North Molton. The many fine Georgian and Victorian houses, particularly the grand 18th-century Guildhall and 19th-century Assembly Rooms, were built with profits from wool and minerals. The 15th-century church has a medieval stone pulpit and handsome figure carvings in the nave.

Refreshments

Old Coaching Inn PH 🍺 *and others in* South Molton
Sportsmans Inn PH, Sandyway Cross
Poltimore Arms PH, North Molton

Quince Honey Farm, South Molton 1

Wild Exmoor honeybees live here in their natural habitats. This is Britain's largest working honey farm and includes press-button hives that open to reveal the centre of the colony.

North Devon Farm Park, Swimbridge 7

Rare breeds of cattle, sheep, poultry and waterfowl roam the 25 acres of this park.

Mole's Chamber

Kinsford Gate

Sandyway Cross

Holywell Cross

North Molton

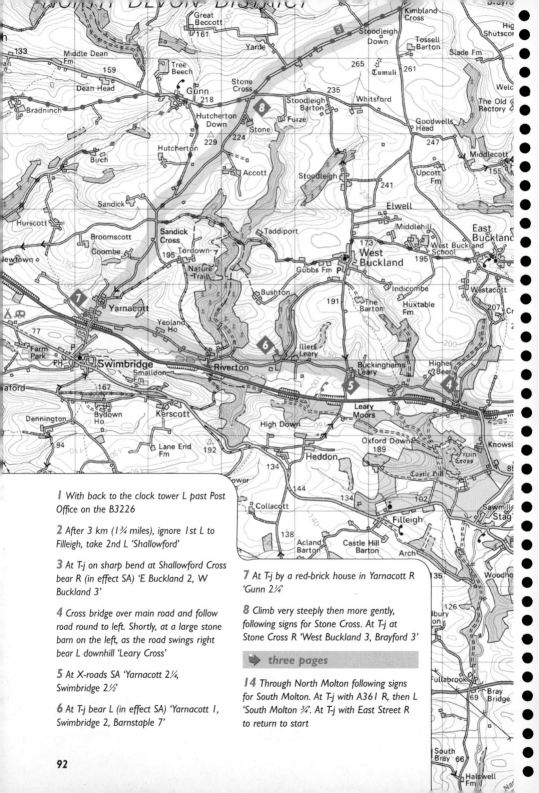

1 With back to the clock tower L past Post Office on the B3226

2 After 3 km (1¾ miles), ignore 1st L to Filleigh, take 2nd L 'Shallowford'

3 At T-j on sharp bend at Shallowford Cross bear R (in effect SA) 'E Buckland 2, W Buckland 3'

4 Cross bridge over main road and follow road round to left. Shortly, at a large stone barn on the left, as the road swings right bear L downhill 'Leary Cross'

5 At X-roads SA 'Yarnacott 2¼, Swimbridge 2½'

6 At T-j bear L (in effect SA) 'Yarnacott 1, Swimbridge 2, Barnstaple 7'

7 At T-j by a red-brick house in Yarnacott R 'Gunn 2¼'

8 Climb very steeply then more gently, following signs for Stone Cross. At T-j at Stone Cross R 'West Buckland 3, Brayford 3'

➡ **three pages**

14 Through North Molton following signs for South Molton. At T-j with A361 R, then L 'South Molton ¾'. At T-j with East Street R to return to start

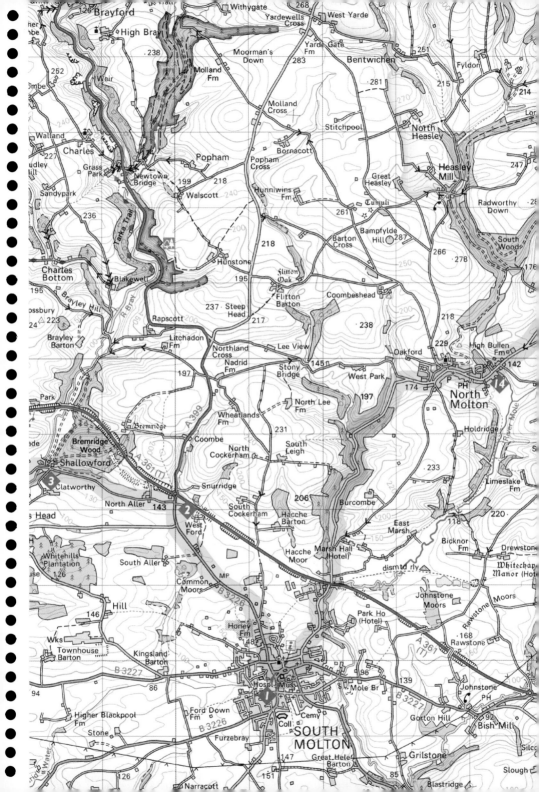

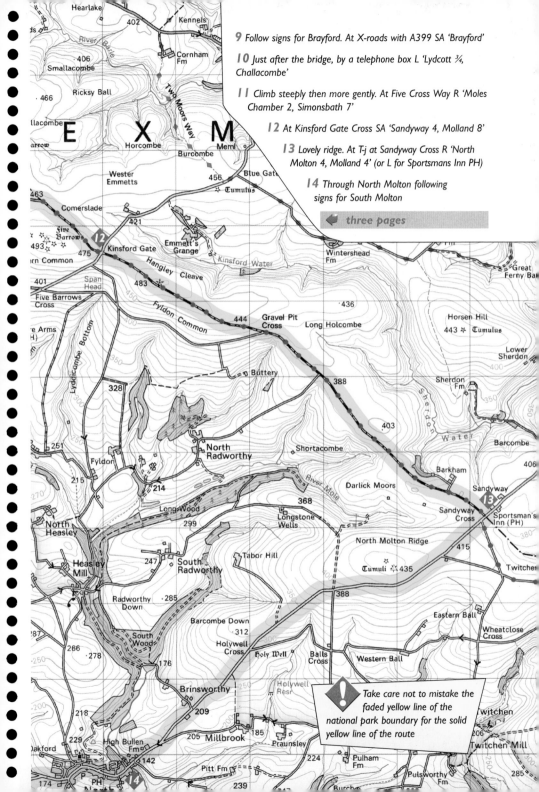

9 Follow signs for Brayford. At X-roads with A399 SA 'Brayford'

10 Just after the bridge, by a telephone box L 'Lydcott ¾, Challacombe'

11 Climb steeply then more gently. At Five Cross Way R 'Moles Chamber 2, Simonsbath 7'

12 At Kinsford Gate Cross SA 'Sandyway 4, Molland 8'

13 Lovely ridge. At T-j at Sandyway Cross R 'North Molton 4, Molland 4' (or L for Sportsmans Inn PH)

14 Through North Molton following signs for South Molton

← three pages

Take care not to mistake the faded yellow line of the national park boundary for the solid yellow line of the route

Corfe Castle to Worth Matravers via Brenscombe Hill and the Priests Way

Start

Bankes Arms Hotel, Corfe Castle

🅿 Large car park on street leading from opposite Bankes Arms Hotel

Distance and grade

21 and 6½ km (13 and 4 miles).
(Total 27 km, 17 miles)

Moderate/strenuous

A ride along two ridges, the first longer, steeper and higher, takes you over Brenscombe Hill and Nine Barrow Down with magnificent views across Poole Harbour, out to the sea and down into the valley. A thrilling descent drops you at the road. Several instructions and junctions later find you at the start of Priest's Way. This starts in a somewhat disjointed fashion with a surfeit of gates, but soon improves. The pub at Worth Matravers is quite a curiosity. The detour to St Alban's Head is certainly worth the effort for more superb views and a look at an amazing little chapel. The return brings the dramatic outline of Corfe Castle closer and closer, finishing with a game of 'dodge the gorse bush' over Corfe Common.

Corfe Castle

Brenscombe Hill

Ulwell

Langton Matravers

Terrain

A steady climb of 180 m (600 ft) from Corfe Castle to the top of Nine Barrow Down, and 110 m (350 ft) from the railway bridge at the bottom of the valley to the highpoint of Priest's Way near Eastington Farm

 ## Nearest railway

Wareham, 8 km (5 miles) northwest of Corfe Castle

 ## Places of interest

Corfe Castle

From its construction by William the Conquerer to its destruction by Parliamentary forces in the Civil War, Corfe Castle has witnessed many episodes in English history. Williams I's son, Robert, Duke of Normandy, was imprisoned here; King John, whose favourite castle it was, imprisoned his wife here in 1212 and four years later hid his crown and treasures here; Edward II, who improved and enlarged the castle, was imprisoned in it in 1326. Henry VII visited in 1496, and in 1571 Elizabeth I sold the castle to Sir Christopher Hatton, whose widow later disposed it of to the Royalist Sir John Bankes. Sir John spent most of his time in attendance on Charles I, and when the Civil War broke out, Lady Bankes was left to defend the castle. She held out bravely but was eventually defeated, and in 1646 the House of Commons voted to demolish the building.

 ## Refreshments

Lots of good pubs and tea shops in **Corfe Castle** *Square and Compass PH* 🍴🍷*, tea shop,* **Worth Matravers**

Worth Matravers

St Alban's Head

Worth Matravers

Afflington Farm

1 With your back to the Bankes Arms Hotel R on A351 towards Wareham, then 1st R onto Sandy Hill Lane under railway bridge (11'6")

2 On RH bend, just past Challow Farm House on your right and Challow Car Park on your left, turn L on track 'Ulwell 3¾'

3 Fork L 'Ridge Path, Rollington Hill ½, Ulwell 3½'

4 Near the top of the hill by mast at X-roads of tracks SA 'Ulwell 2¾'

5 Continue on main track over Allwood Down towards top of hill, following signs for Ulwell then Swanage and Studland

6 Following signs for Ulwell again, just before mast by a gate and a fence bear R onto broad downhill track

7 Superb descent to road. R then 1st R by Ulwell Cottage 'Caravan Site'

8 Just past thatched cottage by water pump 1st road R

9 At T-j under telephone wires R, then after 800 m (½ mile), shortly after Godlingston Farm on the right, 1st road L opposite low stone wall

10 At A351 R, then L on Days Road. Climb to brow of hill. Just past Casterbridge Close on your left, turn R onto tarmac track opposite Benlease Way (between houses no 74 and 76)

11 After 50 m (yd), 1st track L then shortly R onto Priest's Way 'Worth 3¼'

12 Go to the right of the ruin, through gate and SA through next gate

13 **Easy to miss** After passing through a series of gates, before losing height, keep an eye out for cattle grid on left. Cross grid on track towards grey stone farm 'South Barn'. Follow track around the back of the farmhouse 'Priest's Way'

14 Bear L of the barn ahead and follow Priest's Way in same direction for 3 km (2 miles), the final section being across a grazed field (the middle part of this 3 km (2 mile) stretch may be muddy)

15 At road L. Follow road past Square and Compass PH. (If you do not wish to go to St Alban's Head, turn R here and follow the second half of instruction 17.) If you are doing the full ride, carry on past tea shop towards church

16 At Renscombe Farm, on sharp RH bend L 'Bridleway to St Aldhelm's Head'

17 Go as far as chapel and return to the PH. Just before PH, bear L 'Kingston 2, Corfe Castle 4, Wareham 8'

18 At T-j with B3069 L 'Kingston 1, Corfe Castle 3, Wareham 7½', then R on track opposite farm 'Bridleway'.

19 Steep descent, muddy near gate by farm. Follow track between barns then swing L after barns. At road L, then L again on RH bend (chevrons) just past Peak House on left. 'National Trust, Corfe Common'

20 Wiggle your way through gorse, bearing slightly R. At road SA through another bridle gate 'Corfe Common'. Contour and bear slightly R across open common aiming towards distinctive chalk track climbing hill ahead to join road. R on road to return to Corfe Castle

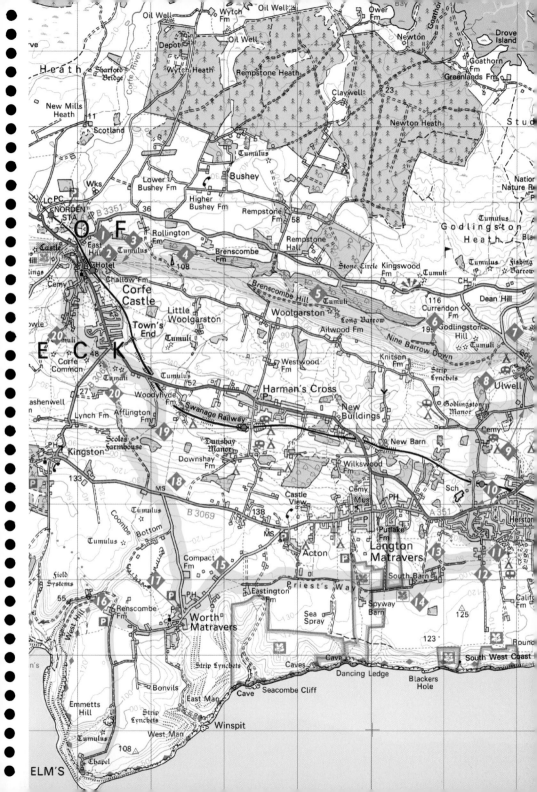

Corfe Castle southwest to Swyre Head, returning via Knowle Hill

Here is a short ride packed with all the best ingredients: challenging climbs on firm surfaces, woodland, panoramic views from Swyre Head – the highest point on the Dorset coast – broad tracks over chalk downland, a tricky descent and an open grassy descent, and not too much mud. And then there are the cream teas to look forward to back in Corfe Castle. Particularly satisfying is the way you can see the whole course of the ride from either of the two ridges that form the northern and southern side of the route.

Refreshments

Several good pubs and tea shops in **Corfe Castle**

Start

Bankes Arms Hotel, Corfe Castle

P Large car park on street leading from opposite Bankes Arms Hotel

Distance and grade

19 km (12 miles)

Moderate/strenuous

Terrain

Two climbs, one of 200 m (650 ft) from Corfe Castle to Swyre Head on tarmac and good tracks, particularly steep near Blashenwell Farm; the second of 140 m (450 ft) from the bottom of Steeple Hill to Grange Arch, also on tarmac and good tracks

Nearest railway

Wareham, 8 km (5 miles) northwest of Corfe Castle

Corfe Castle

Blashenwell Farm

Kingston

Swyre Head

Kimmeridge

Isle of Purbeck

Designated an area of outstanding natural beauty, the Isle of Purbeck is a lovely peninsula that stretches from Poole Harbour to Lulworth Cave with the Purbeck Hills to the west.

▲ *Smedmore Hill above Kimmeridge*

Kingston 5

Kingston's 19th-century church is thought to be one of the best in the area; notable features are the black Purbeck marble pillars and the stone-vaulted chancel.

Kimmeridge and Smedmore House 7

This small village with thatched and slate-roofed cottages lies near a bay renowned for fossils. The Smedmore Estate owns the bay and all the land round the village, and the manor house is open to the public. Construction of the house began in the 1620s but the architecture is a mixture of styles ranging from Jacobean to Queen Anne and Georgian. Dutch furniture and paintings are on display and there is a collection of antique dolls.

Grange Arch 10–11

Now known as Bond's Folly, this arch was built by Denis Bond in about 1740 as an imposing entrance to his house Creech Grange. There are excellent views, sometimes as far as the Isle of Portland.

Steeple Hill   Grange Arch   Ridgeway Hill   Knowle Hill

1 With your back to Bankes Arms Hotel SA towards National Trust shop, following road round to left 'Car Park' (Or from the car park, follow the exit road, at T-j R and join instruction 2)

2 At end of road SA onto no through road 'Blashenwell Farm Only'

3 Follow road to farm and R at the end of the farmyard 'Willwood House' (blue arrow)

4 Bear L at fork of tracks steeply uphill to T-j of tracks. L into wood. At X-roads of tracks in wood SA

5 At road R. Follow this as far as signposts for Encombe Farms, Orchard Hill Farm. At this point L through stone pillars, then R 'No cars, bridlepath only'

6 Follow track gently uphill to Swyre Head, then sharply R along fence

7 After 2½ km (1½ miles) at road L, then at T-j R and after 20 m (yd) L through bridlegate 'Range Walks, Steeple Leaze'

8 Shortly after next metal gate diagonally R up over brow of hill to your right towards gate in fence (no obvious track). If you miss this, and you find yourself by the firing range flagpost, head back towards the gate in fence diagonally to your left

9 Descend on stony track (at times technical) to farm. Climb on track/tarmac to road. Turn L 'Steeple and Creech Hill, Army Ranges'. Steeply to top and follow road round to R 'Wareham 4½. Alternative route to Lulworth'

10 Just beyond flagpole by Steeple Picnic Area and car park R, then L onto track parallel with road 'Grange Arch ½, Corfe Castle 3½'

11 Keep an eye open for bridlegate on left to join track on other side of fence 'Cocknowle ½, Corfe Castle 2¼'

12 At road R, then L (both in effect SA) 'Ridge Path. Corfe Castle 1¾'

13 Continue on track in same direction past Mary Baxter Commemoration Stone and past wood on left, following stone markers for Corfe, eventually descending on fast track

14 At road L. At A351 R 'Swanage'

Chalk ridges near the Dorset coast southeast from Dorchester

Dorset seems to be blessed with a much higher proportion of good-quality bridleways than most other counties in southern England. This ride uses those that follow the ridges on the chalk hills between Weymouth and Lulworth. The ride climbs from Broadmayne to join the Dorset Coast Path over White Horse Hill. It follows the ridge to the main road and soon you lose all your height before you embark on a steep road climb to the top of the white cliffs of Dorset. This stretch offers some magnificent views out to sea and along the coast. Thirsty? There is an excellent pub in East Chaldon. The return half follows the ridge along the inland hills on much rougher, grassier terrain. Swooping down to the A352, the terrain changes to a much softer agricultural character amid woodland. And then, of course, there is the ford.

 Start

Osmington Drove, Broadmayne. 6½ km (4 miles) southeast of Dorchester on the A352, 1st R after the stores/post office

P Limited parking at the start (see above). Larger car park at the end of the lane signposted 'Ringstead' off the A353 (instruction 7), but this will leave you with a steep climb at the finish

 Distance and grade

29 km (18 miles)

🡒🡒🡒🡒
Moderate/strenuous

Broadmayne

White Horse Hill

Upton

Daggers G

Terrain

Four climbs: 110 m (350 feet) from Broadmayne to White Horse Hill on firm tracks; 100 m (330 feet) from the A353 to the car park on top of the cliffs, mainly on tarmac; 51 m (170 feet) from near the car park to the obelisk, at times rough; 76 m (250 feet) from East Chaldon to Moigns Down, mostly on tarmac but the ridge can be rough

Nearest railway

Dorchester, 6½ km (4 miles) from Broadmayne

Refreshments

Black Dog PH, **Broadmayne**
Sailors Return PH 🍴🍴,
East Chaldon

East Chaldon
Five Marys

Watercombe

Warmwell

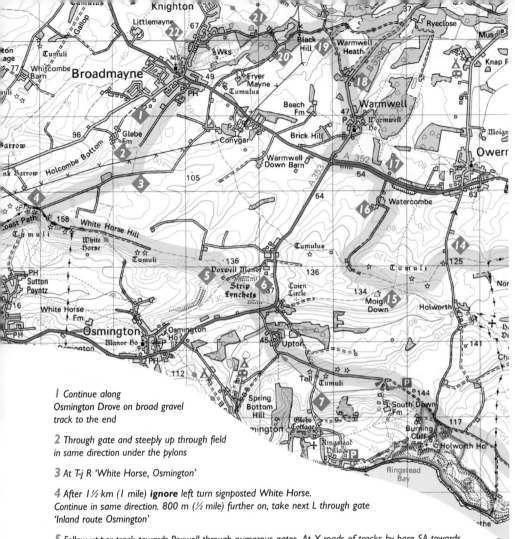

1 Continue along
Osmington Drove on broad gravel
track to the end

2 Through gate and steeply up through field
in same direction under the pylons

3 At T-j R 'White Horse, Osmington'

4 After 1½ km (1 mile) **ignore** left turn signposted White Horse.
Continue in same direction. 800 m (½ mile) further on, take next L through gate
'Inland route Osmington'

5 Follow upper track towards Poxwell through numerous gates. At X-roads of tracks by barn SA towards
gate set against skyline, then through next field to the R of telegraph pole you can see from the gate

6 Head towards small wood and buildings. Descend to busy A353. **Extreme care – dangerous crossing**: it is best
to go left for 100 m (yd) to give yourself a clear view before crossing the road. Turn R on road then 1st L
'Ringstead 1½'

7 Follow this road in same direction up steep hill, through car park then gate 'West Lulworth 5. No cars please'

8 Continue in same direction along track then field edges then track again for 5½ km (3½ miles) following signs for
Daggers Gate. Wonderful views

9 At bottom of hill, 50 m (yd) **before** reaching road L uphill towards barn (blue arrow)

10 At next barn R 'East Chaldon'. At gate L down into valley 'East Chaldon'. (Short rough section). Follow blue
arrows and waymarks to road

11 At road L, then follow it to the right around village green, past Sailors Return PH

12 At top of steep hill, on RH bend L through gate 'White Horse Hill 4½'

13 Through several gates in same direction to road. At road SA

14 Through several more gates. At next road SA

15 Across open field towards gate in hedgerow 400 m (¼ mile) ahead. At end of next field, with a stile on your right, L downhill along fence for 70 m (yd) until reaching major track. Turn R through gate downhill towards farm buildings

16 Follow this track past barns and downhill to farm. At X-roads with tarmac next to the farm SA, bearing R around the edge of the buildings

17 Follow drive to A352 (busy road). L towards the roundabout then R onto B3390 'Affpuddle. Crossways. Warmwell' (**Take care** - if in doubt about negotiating the roundabout, dismount and cross each road individually)

18 Through Warmwell. After 400 m (yd), on RH bend, shortly after New Cottage on your right L 'Private road. Speed limit 15mph. Public bridleway only'

19 After 800 m (½ mile) at start of woodland on the left leave tarmac and turn L onto track between trees

20 At a triangular mud/earth clearing, beneath a telephone line, before the farm R on track downhill

21 Through the ford (clean your bike?) At T-j L

22 This track becomes tarmac. At T-j at the end of Watergates Lane L. At A352 SA, then 1st L on Cowleaze Road to return to start

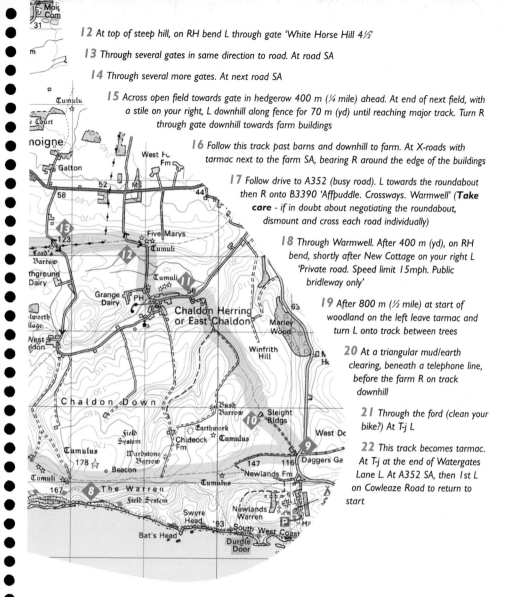

From Dorchester via Maiden Castle and Hardy Monument to Abbotsbury

A superb breezy ride over the chalk downland southwest of Dorchester, the route takes in fine sea views and a good refuelling stop at Abbotsbury. It starts by skirting the base of the impressive hill fort of Maiden Castle before joining the Dorset Coast Path along the broad ridge track to Hardy Monument, where there are panoramic views out to sea and over the Dorset hills. A swift descent through woodland brings you to Portesham and along a disused railway to Abbotsbury – a good place to stop before a very steep climb up onto White Hill. Flint and chalk tracks and quiet lanes take you up over the ridge and down into the valley of the River Frome. A final climb from Muckleford to cross the busy A35 drops you in Martinstown, close to Maiden Castle and Dorchester.

 Start

Roundabout at the west end of High Street West, Dorchester

P Follow signs in Dorchester or start at Maiden Castle

 Distance and grade

44 km (28 miles)

Strenuous

 Terrain

Four major climbs : 170 m (550 ft) from Dorchester to Hardy Monument, 150 m (500 ft) from Abbotsbury on to White Hill, 150 m (500 ft) from Long Bredy to the Roman Road on the ridge and 91 m (300 ft) from Muckleford south to the A35

 Nearest railway

Dorchester

1 From the roundabout take Albert Road southwards out of town 'Weymouth A354'. This becomes Cornwall Road. At 1st traffic lights SA onto Maumbury Road

2 At 2nd traffic lights R 'Weymouth', then 3rd R onto Maiden Castle Road 'Maiden Castle 1½'

3 From the car park, take the main track towards the RH edge of the hill. At the 2nd gate leave the main track, turn R uphill through field for 50 m (yd) to join less well-defined track, which continues uphill on the RH side of the fence

4 Over the brow of the hill, through the field on main track and exit via gate onto road. Turn R, then at T-j with B3159 L 'Upwey, Weymouth'

5 Climb for 1½ km (1 mile). At brow of hill R through gateway onto track 'No vehicles please'

 three pages

28 A T-j at bottom R, then after 30 m (yd) R again 'Muckleford 1¼'

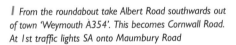

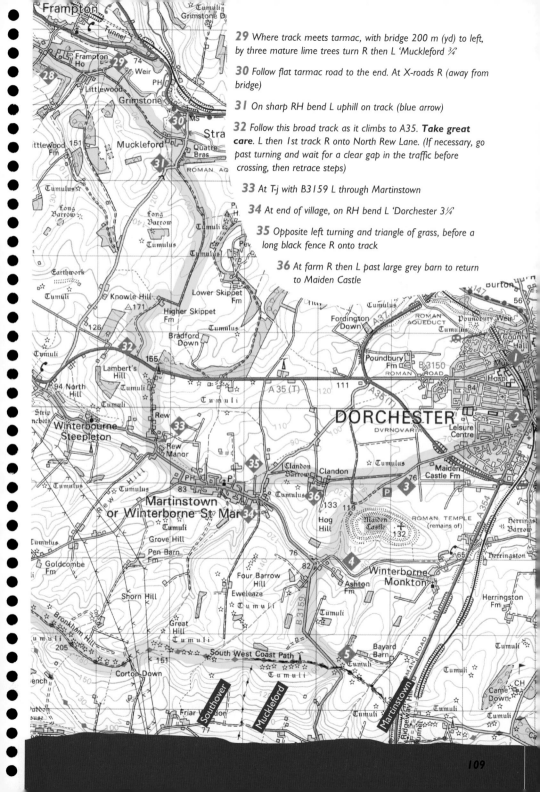

29 Where track meets tarmac, with bridge 200 m (yd) to left, by three mature lime trees turn R then L 'Muckleford ¾'

30 Follow flat tarmac road to the end. At X-roads R (away from bridge)

31 On sharp RH bend L uphill on track (blue arrow)

32 Follow this broad track as it climbs to A35. **Take great care**. L then 1st track R onto North Rew Lane. (If necessary, go past turning and wait for a clear gap in the traffic before crossing, then retrace steps)

33 At T-j with B3159 L through Martinstown

34 At end of village, on RH bend L 'Dorchester 3¼'

35 Opposite left turning and triangle of grass, before a long black fence R onto track

36 At farm R then L past large grey barn to return to Maiden Castle

▲ Maiden Castle

6 Follow this track for 5½ km (3½ miles), under pylons and towards Hardy Monument. At road L

7 Shortly after brow of hill L onto forestry track, just before woodland begins

8 Follow main track down through wood. At barn at bottom R uphill towards clump of trees then past barn onto tarmac

9 Fast descent. At T-j with road R, then at T-j in Portesham L towards Kings Arms PH. At T-j with B3157 R 'Abbotsbury 2'

10 **Take care**. After 400 m (¼ mile), immediately after Millmead Country Guest House R onto track

11 Take 2nd R through a black gate just before small black barn onto dismantled railway. At times muddy. Follow to the end

12 At road R into Abbotsbury. Opposite Ilchester Arms PH R up Back Street

13 After 200 m (yd), just past a row of thatched yellow stone cottages, before Spring Cottage, L up track, which becomes very steep

14 Ignore right turn to Lime Kiln, carry SA uphill towards gate at RH edge of hedge

15 At next gate (in hedgerow) bear R uphill 'White Hill'

16 At next waymark R through middle of three gates then L uphill at right angles to the fence (ie directly away from sea)

17 At T-j with major track just before next gates R and follow this as it turns sharply L downhill towards wood. At tarmac L past farm

18 Contour on this track, at times rough, through several fields and gates to emerge at tarmac. Turn R (sign to left 'Private road, Bridleway over Private Property')

19 Climb steeply. As gradient flattens, take LH fork downhill, ignoring turns

20 In Long Bredy near a cluster of houses SA at junction with road, following signs for the church

21 400 m (¼ mile) after passing no through road to church 1st R 'Dorchester 8½'

22 At T-j with A35 SA (white 'T' sign)

23 Go past buildings, ignore right turn by green barn, continue climbing gently. At T-j with lane R

24 At next T-j L 'Compton Valence 1, Maiden Newton 3½'

25 800 m (½ mile) after the turning to Compton Valence, take the next R on a broad stony track by a lonesome tree

26 Follow along several field edges (Dorset County Council blue arrows). Rough in parts. Track becomes enclosed

27 At tarmac L downhill away from farm

28 A T-j at bottom R, then after 30 m (yd) R again 'Muckleford 1¼'

◁ two pages

Places of interest

Maiden Castle

This hilltop site has been intermittently occupied for about five thousand years. The earliest inhabitants were late Stone-Age people of the Windmill Hill culture who settled at the eastern end of Maiden Castle. Iron Age dwellers were present from about 350BC and occupied a much larger area, eventually amounting to 45 acres. They progressively strengthened and elaborated their defences by enlarging and adding to the ramparts and ditches, and constructing winding, well-protected entrances of timber, stone and earth. However, Maiden Castle failed to withstand the invading Roman forces who stormed it in 43 AD. Archeologists have uncovered the graves of the defenders, many of whose skeletons show damage inflicted by sword-cuts or the missiles hurled by Roman ballistae.

5 *The Mendips north of Wells*

*T*he route for this energetic ride at the eastern end of the Mendips starts from the historic town of Wells and passes through the equally famous Wookey Hole. After a stiff road climb, you reach a ridge that provides panoramic views. A fast descent, part on-road, part off-road and semi-technical, leaves you at the start of the second climb – this time off-road. When you regain the ridge, there is a short-road section on quiet lanes before a last, lovely descent through Dinder Wood back to Wells. There is a short section on a footpath across a field, which saves you from dropping down into and climbing back up from Wells and also avoids the busy A39. You must get off your bike and walk this 400 m (¼ mile) section.

Start

Centre of Wells

P Follow signs from the centre of Wells

Distance and grade

26 km (16 miles)

🌶🌶🌶🌶🌶 Strenuous

Terrain

Two steep climbs up onto the Mendips, one on-road and one off-road. Farm tracks, woodland tracks

Nearest railway

Castle Cary, 16 km (10 miles) southeast of Wells or Highbridge, 19 km (12 miles) west of Wells

---

Off-road riding tips

● If using a jet spray to clean your bike, do not aim the hose directly at the hubs or bottom bracket but clean these parts from above

● Lubricate your bike after washing it or after a very wet ride, paying particular attention to the chain

Wells

Wookey Hole

Rookham

Walcombe

Wells 1

Situated at the foot of the Mendip Hills, Wells is one of the smallest cathedral cities in England. Apart from its spectacular West Front, the cathedral is worth a visit to see the 14th-century astronomical clock and the chapter house.

Wookey Hole 3

Famous caverns worn away over thousands of years by the River Axe, which can be heard rushing far below deep into the caves. There are no spectacular rock formations but the caverns are immense and there are relics of pre-historic man. Nearby is a mill dating back to the 17th-century that still produces hand-made paper.

Refreshments

*Plenty of choice in **Wells and Wookey Hole**
Hunters Lodge Inn 🍺, **Priddy** (1½ km (1 mile)
north of the route at instruction 6)
Slab House Inn, **on the B3139** at
instruction 13*

Haydon

East Horrington

1 Head out of town along Chamberlain Street

2 R at Whiting Way, L along Mountery Road then R on to Wookey Hole Road

3 Go through Wookey Hole, bearing R at a fork 'Single Track Road'

4 After a steep climb, as the road flattens out, 100 m (yd) after passing a white house with a conservatory on your left, turn R on a track 'Ebbor Grove, Dursdon Drove'

5 Follow this track in the same direction for 4 km (2½ miles). It changes surface several times from farmtrack to grassy track and everything in between. 'No Cycling' signs will tell you where you must not ride. The surface eventually turns to tarmac and brings you to a T-j with the road

6 R steeply downhill, but do not lose all your height. After about 800 m (½ mile), as views start to open up on your right, opposite a sort of lay-by with gates on your right, turn L up a track past Ivy Cottage 'Bridleway'

7 Shortly, fork R down a narrow track. Although this track seems unlikely, it **is** a bridleway. A semi-technical descent through a mossy sunken lane brings you to road

(This adventurous track can at times be overgrown, muddy, rutted, stony, unrideable. If you wish to avoid this section, follow the road down, taking 1st L turn, rejoining route at second part of instruction 8)

8 At the road L. After 50 m (yd) L again, then at a T-j L a 3rd time

9 On a sharp RH bend L by two metal garage doors

10 After 60 m (yd) leave main track to go R over a stile. This 400 m (¼ mile) section is a **footpath**, so **walk** the bike diagonally L to the top LH corner of the field by a white house and a stone-built house

11 Leave the field and turn L up track, following blue arrows and climbing steeply. Turn R on tarmac at the top

12 At X-roads with road SA 'Lower Haydon Farm'

13 Follow instructions carefully as there are few signposts on this road section: at T-j L then 1st R. At next T-j R, then at X-roads L 'Chilcote, Dinder'

14 At T-j R by The Beeches house. Pass the manor house and take the next R

15 Ignore track to right over cattle grid. Follow tarmac to gate. **Do not** follow main track to left, but follow the hedge-row to your right on firm grass

16 Follow the track in this direction, bearing R when necessary, until the field narrows between woodland

17 Steeply down through woodland, through gate and fork L. At T-j with the B3139 R (use pavement with discretion to avoid the main road). Shortly after the Fountain Inn turn L to go past the cathedral and return to the start

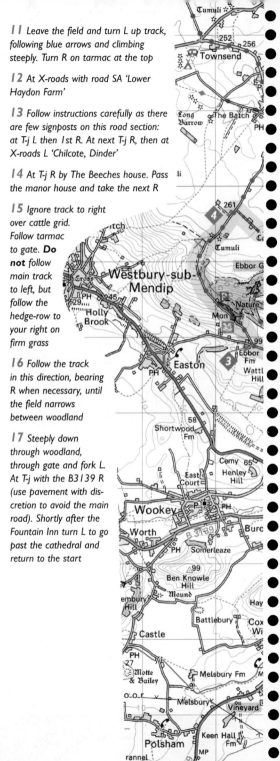

A slice of Cheddar and a taste of the Mendips

The Carboniferous limestone of the Mendips provides a marked contrast to the surrounding countryside. The ride climbs the Mendips twice, offering panoramic views across the Bristol Channel and over the Somerset Levels and moors. There are two steep descents, one narrow and stony through woodland, the other somewhat broader, through forestry plantation. The top ridge may be muddy. The area is also popular with walkers and horses, so show consideration, letting others pass and thanking them when they let you pass.

 ## Places of interest

Cheddar Gorge 1

The famous gorge is actually a collapsed cavern and runs for approximately 1½ km (1 mile) to the north-east of the village. The thickly wooded slopes and cliffs rise up to 460 m (1500 ft) above the roadway. Much of the area is owned by the National Trust. Roman coins and remains of prehistoric man have been found in the caves in the gorge, some of which are open to the public.

Burrington Combe 6

Another gorge, less spectacular than Cheddar. Augustus Toplady (1740–78) wrote the lines of the famous hymn 'Rock of ages cleft for me' while sheltering from a storm here.

 ## Start

The Edelweiss Restaurant, opposite the Cheddar Caves Information Booth at the lower end of Cheddar's main street

P The nearer the centre of Cheddar, the more expensive the car parks

 ## Distance and grade

29 km (18 miles)

Strenuous

 ## Terrain

Two steep climbs from north and south of the Mendips. Forest tracks, open moorland, farm tracks

 ## Nearest railway

Yatton, 10 km (6 miles) from the route at Rowberrow

Cheddar

King Down Farm

Beacon Batch

▲ Cheddar Gorge

Read's Cavern

Refreshments

Lots of choice in **Cheddar**
The Swan PH 🍺, **Rowberrow**
(just off the route between
instructions 7 and 8)

1 From the Edelweiss Restaurant, take the minor road out of Cheddar (to the left of St Andrews Road)

2 Pass Cheddar driving range on your left. At T-j L for 300 m (yd) as far as signpost for Hilltops B&B. L then R, leaving Bradley Cottage on your left

3 Follow this grassy track towards copse, following blue arrows and signs for Daycott. Continue uphill through gate with two large wooden posts. Climb steeply on narrow stony track, then more gently on broad farm track through several gates, eventually descending to the road

4 At X-roads with road (B3135) SA 'Compton Martin, Harptree'. After 1½ km (1 mile) 1st road L 'Charterhouse'. At X-roads near to Charterhouse church SA, then after 800 m (½ mile) 1st L on bridleway towards masts

5 Keep to left of mast. At trig point, continue in same direction towards top corner of plantation. At T-j of bridleways R then L to wood. There will be muddy stretches at all times of the year on the 3-km (2-miles) section between the masts and the start of the wood. These will be at their worst from winter to late spring. The two alternatives are: drop down on the road through Burrington Combe then cut southwest to rejoin the route beneath Dolebury Warren **or**, for a shorter ride, follow the road from the X-roads at Charterhouse to Tynings Farm and rejoin the route at instruction 10

6 Straight descent through wood to gap between poles. After 50 m (yd), at X-roads of tracks L on good stony track through woodland

7 After 1½ km (1 mile), in a small clearing with a green gate ahead and left of you turn L, passing a field, then stables on your right. (Keep a sharp eye out for this instruction)

8 Pass the pink, white and cream houses on your left, keeping to unmetalled track. At X-roads of bridleways SA, following blue arrow signs for Cheddar

9 Cross stream to your left and join forestry track coming up from the left. At X-roads of tracks SA to Tyning's Farm. Through farm to road

10 At road SA, with wall on your right. After 300 m (yd), as road bends R, SA 'Road unsuitable for motor vehicles'

11 Where this bears L into quarry SA down steep bridlepath into Cheddar. In open field, take the broad track to the L and follow main track as it bends round to T-j with road

12 R on road (Hannay Road) then 1st L (Kent Street) to return to start

Around Wimbleball Lake, Exmoor

*T*he two loops of this ride to the south of the Brendon Hills give you the option of three rides of different lengths.

The southern loop 16 km (10 miles) takes the track east from the dam through woods to the B3190, cuts back west on road to the car park at Haddon Hill, then descends on an amazing, steep, sunken track that is at times overgrown, muddy, rutted, stony or unrideable but always beautiful and a real adventure. If this sounds a bit rough, then there is an alternative descent by road to the ford at Bury to rejoin the route. The next part is the best of the whole trip as the route follows the River Haddeo along Hartford Bottom, then on Lady Harriet's Drive on broad tracks back to the dam beneath the lake. A very steep climb takes you up on to the dam and back to the car park.

The northern and easier loop 11 km (7 miles) follows the edge of Wimbleball Lake before climbing 76 m (250 ft) to the remains of St James Church on Upton Hill. Having descended to Upton, the ride retraces the outward route of the southern loop on the track that runs westwards along the bottom edge of the lake to cross the dam and return to the car park. There are fine views all around this loop.

 ### Start

Wimbleball Lake Water Park, 6½ km (4 miles) south of the B3224 between Bishops Lydeard and Wheddon Cross. Alternatively, Haddon Hill car park on the B3190 east of Dulverton

P As above

 ### Distance and grade

11 and 16 km (7 and 10 miles) (two loops total 27 km (17 miles)) ✏ to ✏✏✏✏✏ according to which loops are chosen

Terrain

From easy tracks to technical descents. One short, very steep climb on road just south of the dam and a more gentle one from the north end of the lake up to Upton Farm, part on-road, part off-road

 ### Nearest railway

Tiverton Parkway, 26 km (16 miles) to the southeast

Higher Cowlings

Dam

Haddon Farm

Hartford

Places of interest

Wimbleball Lake Water Park *16*
374 acres of water and 500 acres of surrounding woodland and meadow. Tea rooms situated in the park.

▲ *Wimbleball Lake*

Dam   Rugg's Farm   Venne Cott   Upton Farm   Upton   Dam

Loop 1

1 Out of Wimbleball Lake Water Park and turn L

2 Shortly after reaching the brow of the hill, by triangle of grass, R uphill 'Hartford, Haddon Hill'

3 Keep bearing L towards dam. Cross bridge, L on Lady Harriet's Drive 'Upton 1¾'

4 1st L on Lady Harriet's Drive 'Upton 1½' (the track from Haddon Hill car park joins the route at this point)

5 Stay on main, lower track through woodland through several gates to road

6 At road R

7 After 1½ km (1 mile), on sharp LH bend (Haddon Hill car park on right) SA on track just to the left of a white house. (If you do not fancy the steep, rough off-road descent, follow road to X-roads, turn R and rejoin route at ford)

8 At farm buildings by Haddon Farm bear L towards sunken grassy track. Good luck!

Loop 2

16 From the information centre in the car park go straight downhill towards the lake on a grassy track by the hedgerow

17 Near the lake L, following signs for Bessom Bridge. At X-roads with tarmac lane SA passing a wooden hut on your right

18 At road R to cross bridge

19 1st R 'Upton 2½, Wiveliscombe 8½'

20 Climb steeply. Ignore 1st R to Lower Holworthy Farm. Take next R 'No Through Road'

21 At the T-j by the ruins of the church L

22 At T-j by Rainsbury House bear R downhill (in effect SA)

23 At T-j with B3190 R 'Bampton 6, Dulverton 6'

24 Just after white cottage on left, ignore footpath to the right, take next R through wide wooden gate L 'Hartford 2, Dam 1½'

25 At fork of tracks with the lake visible to the right, bear L on upper, more major track. Retracing route, at T-j R 'Wimbleball Dam ¼, Bury 2¾'

26 Over dam and L to return to water park

9 Follow track onto tarmac. At T-j with road, near telephone box, R

10 Through ford or over bridge. Bear R, past Old School House, down no through road

11 SA through white wooden gate, past lodge 'Bridleway to Hartford 2, Upton 4¾'

12 After 3 km (2 miles), at junction of tracks, L 'Upton 2½, Haddon Hill, Dam, avoiding houses'

13 After 300 m (yd) R through wooden gate over bridge

14 Shortly after 2nd gate, fork R very steeply uphill

15 Cross bridge, L 'Brompton Regis 2¼' retrace route back to car park bearing L at T-j with road by triangle of grass then after 1 km (¾ mile) R over cattle grid 'Wimbleball Park, Main Entrance'

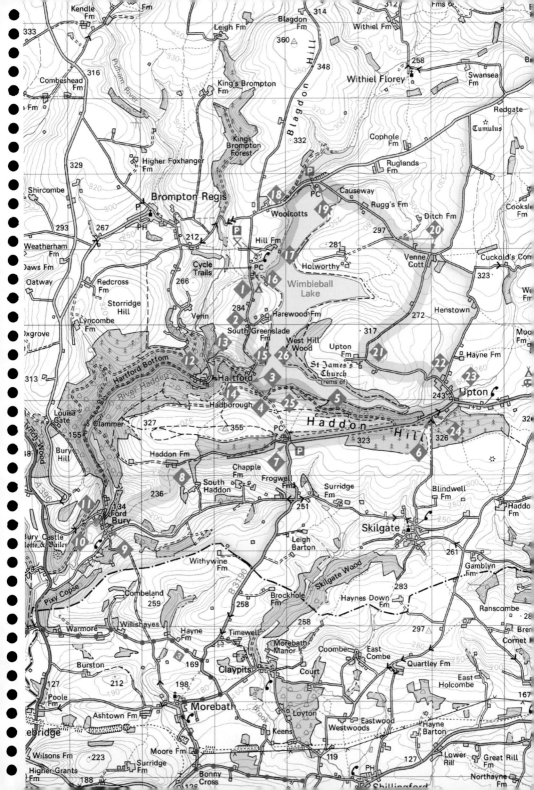

High ridges between three Exmoor villages

Exmoor has a high density of bridleways, offering superb riding almost wherever you choose. This cycle ride links together three of the most picturesque villages on the moor via roads and tracks that are almost all passable year-round. The views are spectacular, as might be expected from a ride with so much climbing. Good refeshment stops are an added delight.

Refreshments

Royal Oak PH 🍺🍺, **Withypool**
Royal Oak PH 🍺, **Winsford**
White Horse 🍺, Crown PH, **Exford**

Start

Exford

🅿 Follow signs in Exford

Distance and grade

29 km (18 miles)
🌶🌶🌶🌶🌶 Strenuous

Terrain

Climbs out of each village: from Exford, a steady road climb; from Withypool, a very steep road climb and from Winsford, a steep climb off-road past Kemps Farm. Two rough sections, one northwest of Withypool, the other near Knaplock; otherwise all year-round tracks

Nearest railway

Tiverton Parkway, 40 km (25 miles)

Off-road riding tips

● The deepest part of a puddle on a farm track is usually where the vehicles' wheels go, so try the higher ground in the middle

Exford   Withypool   Comer's Cross   Knaplock

Exford 1

This is the most important stag-hunting centre on Exmoor and is the base for the Devon and Somerset Stag Hounds.

Withypool 8

This village has one of the two legal commons existing in the Exmoor National Park. South of the village at Withypool Hill, there is a stone circle amongst neolithic burial mounds.

▲ Exmoor

Spire Cross

Winsford

Kemps Farm

Staddon Hill

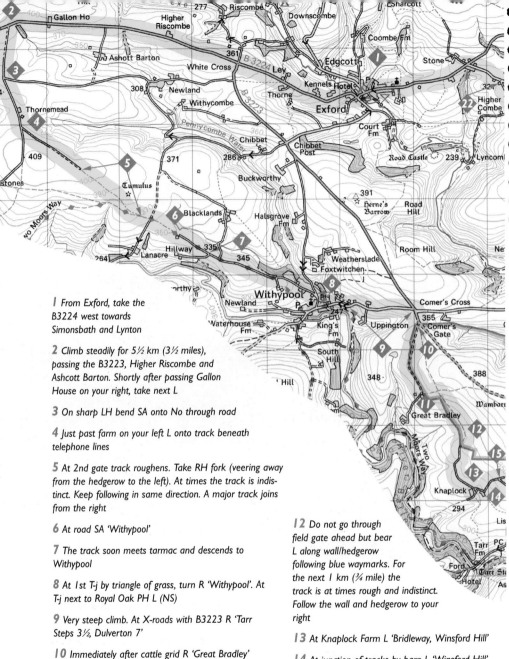

1 From Exford, take the B3224 west towards Simonsbath and Lynton

2 Climb steadily for 5½ km (3½ miles), passing the B3223, Higher Riscombe and Ashcott Barton. Shortly after passing Gallon House on your right, take next L

3 On sharp LH bend SA onto No through road

4 Just past farm on your left L onto track beneath telephone lines

5 At 2nd gate track roughens. Take RH fork (veering away from the hedgerow to the left). At times the track is indistinct. Keep following in same direction. A major track joins from the right

6 At road SA 'Withypool'

7 The track soon meets tarmac and descends to Withypool

8 At 1st T-j by triangle of grass, turn R 'Withypool'. At T-j next to Royal Oak PH L (NS)

9 Very steep climb. At X-roads with B3223 R 'Tarr Steps 3½, Dulverton 7'

10 Immediately after cattle grid R 'Great Bradley'

11 As track bears sharply R downhill over cattle grid turn L, uphill, at T-j of tracks, then bear R 'Tarr Steps via Knaplock'

12 Do not go through field gate ahead but bear L along wall/hedgerow following blue waymarks. For the next 1 km (¾ mile) the track is at times rough and indistinct. Follow the wall and hedgerow to your right

13 At Knaplock Farm L 'Bridleway, Winsford Hill'

14 At junction of tracks by barn L 'Winsford Hill'

15 Bear R, staying on major track 'Winsford via Winsford Hill'

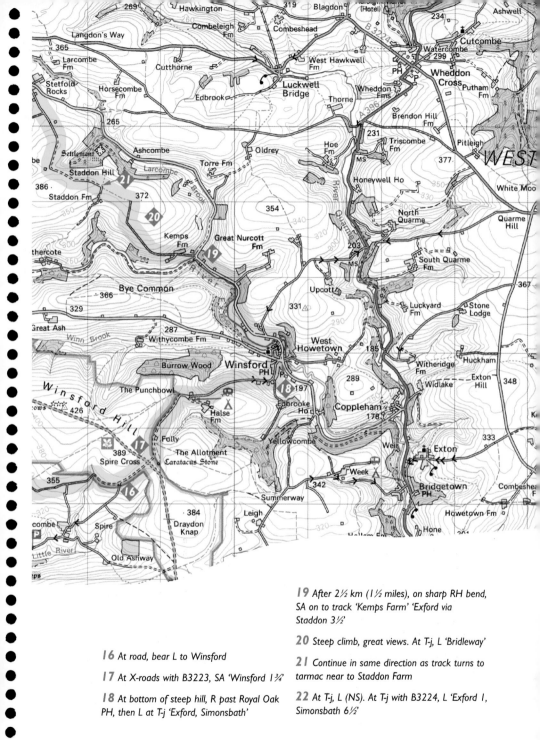

19 After 2½ km (1½ miles), on sharp RH bend, SA on to track 'Kemps Farm' 'Exford via Staddon 3½'

20 Steep climb, great views. At T-j, L 'Bridleway'

21 Continue in same direction as track turns to tarmac near to Staddon Farm

22 At T-j, L (NS). At T-j with B3224, L 'Exford 1, Simonsbath 6½'

16 At road, bear L to Winsford

17 At X-roads with B3223, SA 'Winsford 1¾'

18 At bottom of steep hill, R past Royal Oak PH, then L at T-j 'Exford, Simonsbath'

Useful addresses

British Cycling Federation

National Cycling Centre
Stuart Street
Manchester M11 4DQ
0870 871 2000
www.bcf.uk.com

The BCF co-ordinates and promotes an array of cycle sports and cycling in general. They are a good first point of contact if you want to find out more about how to get involved in cycling. The website provides information on upcoming cycle events and competitions.

CTC (Cyclists Touring Club)

Cotterell House
69 Meadrow
Godalming
Surrey GU7 3HS
01483 417217
www.ctc.org.uk

Britain's largest cycling organisation, promoting recreational and utility cycling. The CTC provides touring and technical advice, legal aid and insurance, and campaigns to improve facilities and opportunities for all cyclists. The website provides details of campaigns and routes and has an online application form.

The London Cycling Campaign

Unit 228
30 Great Guildford Street
London SE1 0HS
020 7928 7220
www.lcc.org.uk

The LCC promotes cycling in London by providing services for cyclists and by campaigning for more facilities for cyclists. Membership of the LCC provides the following benefits: London Cyclist magazine, insurance, legal advice, workshops, organised rides, discounts in bike shops and much more. You can join the LCC on its website.

Sustrans

Head Office
Crown House
37-41 Prince Street
Bristol BS1 4PS
General information line: 0117 929 0888
www.sustrans.org.uk

A registered charity, Sustrans designs and builds systems for sustainable transport. It is best known for its transformation of old railway lines into safe, traffic-free routes for cyclists and pedestrians and wheelchair users. Sustrans is developing the 13,000 km (8000 mile) National Cycle Network on traffic-calmed minor roads and traffic-free paths, to be completed by the year 2005 with major funding from the Millennium Commission.

Veteran Cycle Club

Membership Secretary
31 Yorke Road
Croxley Green
Rickmansworth
Herts WD3 3DW
www.v-cc.org.uk

A very active club, the VCC is concerned with the history and restoration of veteran cycles. Members enjoy organised rides and receive excellent publications relating to cycle history and club news.